THE HOOD NEEDS LOVE, TOO!

A Breath of Liberation &
A Cry of Resistance

Byron D. Brooks

Book production by MysticqueRose Publishing Services LLC

ISBN: 979-8-218-35530-2

CONTENTS

Prelude

Dear reader, as you dive into this literary journey, I want you to keep this thought within your mind, "this book was written by a product of "The Hood!" Now, why would you want me to do that, you may ask?! Throughout numerous decades in America, many within society have negatively stereotyped, belittled, ostracized, and stigmatized "The Hood." When thinking of "The Hood", the average suburbanized American mind quickly thinks of crime, drugs, and a place that should be avoided at all costs.

Due to this heuristic way of thinking, hoods across America and the people who reside therein have been deprived of resources, potential economic growth, and to sum it all up, <u>Love</u>. Our school systems have been structured to create an injustice to children from the hood seeking a well-rounded quality education.

Irrational legislation and political corruption have crippled our communities and put many on an unlevel playing feld within society compared to our suburban counterparts. The late Indian public speaker, Rajneesh, once stated, "Love is power, the purest and the greatest power: Love is God. Nothing can be higher than that but, this power is not a desire to enslave others. This power is not a destructive force.

This power is the very source of creation. This power is creativity, and this power will transform you totally into a new being. It has no concern with anybody. Its whole concern is to bring your seeds to their ultimate flower."

Today, my hope is that in your reading of this book, you will make the conscious decision to shower the hood with love so that its seeds may blossom into equity for all. The Hood included!

Being Black In America

The same Nation that had us singing my Country Tis of Thee
Is the same Nation that kills men, women, boys and girls that
look like me
Being Black in America
For The Past Four Years all I've heard was America scream
about again making it great
and to that notion I beg the question my brothers and sisters
When was our Country truly and ethically great!?
Was it during the time when my people were beaten, enslaved,
and raped!?
Being Black in America
Was it when racist white men filled with hatred burnt crosses
and lynched black and brown Americans
All while wearing a cross across their necks and a white sheet
across their face!?
Being Black in America
Was it when Emit Till was killed based on a white lie
Or when the white woman who admitted she lied was never
tried
Being Black in America
We call this Nation the land of the free and I guess that's true
Well, as long as your skin lacks melanin and your eyes are
deep blue
Being Black in America

Is knowing that if I were to ever step foot ready to riot on
Capitol Hill
I'd be tear gassed, shot and most definitely killed
Yet armed domestic terrorists rioted, stormed, and looted the
building without worry or consequence
All because they had White Privilege as their Shield
Being Black in America
Means that I can be murdered by a White man just for
Jogging in the street
Being Black in America
Means that I can be killed by police right inside my own home
as I sleep
Being Black in America
Means that Justice is swift for everyone except for me
Being Black in America/ Is full of wonderful culture and
Flavor
Being Black in America
Is constantly reminding our Justice system
of the injustice that remains in the Murder of Breanna Taylor!
Being Black in America
Will no longer be a death sentence for my future children
because enough is Enough and I will continue to Fight as long
as the blood within my veins and the Lord all mighty keeps
me living!
Being Black in America
Means taking a stand
Being Black in America
Is showing our oppressors that told us we couldn't
That Yes We Can
On July 23, 1963, in the great city of Detroit, Dr. King for the
first time uttered the words of his Dream
and as a Black man in America Today I do decree

That being Black in America will break the shackles of Power, Privilege, and oppression and finally allow true Freedom to Ring
Being Black In America
Will show our kids that we truly come from Kings and Queens
Being Black in America
Will remove from Our society, Racism, and Hatreds horrible sting Being Black in America will ensure
That All people, no matter the color of their skin nor the place of their origin
Will all be able to live out their American Dream. Being Black in America

- MoSoul

Family

I, like more than half of Black children in the United States, was raised by extended family–my great-grandparents, to be exact. Honestly, it saved my life. Without them, I would have been a ward of the state and eventually ended up in prison or dead. They set me up to live a life of purpose, teaching me lessons and skills and instilling the belief in me that I could achieve things that would have seemed impossible had my vision only been limited to what I saw unfolding in my immediate family. As a child, I was just living life, but as an adult, it's clear to me that family is a backbone, and the one we end up with has the potential to either steady us for growth or damn us to paralysis.

My great-grandmother, JoEsther Corner, was a florist and very strong-willed woman who never bit her tongue when it came to saying what was on her mind. In fact, I inherited my strong will from her, and she created the foundation of my musical talents. When I was four years old, she taught me how to play the piano. I hated it until I found out girls liked it. After that, I loved it, and now I have several music-related degrees. Following his retirement from Eaton Steel, my great-grandfather, Roscoe Corner, was a jitney, which was a rideshare driver before companies like Uber and Lyft were a thing.

I can still remember the fond memories of assisting my "papa," as I would call him, with his duties as a jitney, which entailed taking customers to various grocery stores and helping them carry their groceries into their residences once their shopping was complete. We would partake in a celebratory Three Musketeers candy bar following a successful work day. My grandparents were shining examples of social entrepreneurship before that specific phrase was even coined, and their examples showed me what I could become.

Reflecting on my childhood and upbringing makes it abundantly clear to me that the role of the extended family in the Black community is to fill any necessary gaps in a child's social and self-development and guide the youth towards a path that will empower them to break generational curses. Grandparents, aunts, and uncles play essential roles and hold the power to change the trajectory of one's purpose for better or worse. We should be especially cognizant of the realities of "for better or worse," because what we invest in the next generation will determine what happens to the generations to come.

When we look at the history of Black people in the United States, it's obvious that the goal was never for us to be card-holding citizens, much less to thrive. The reason we've been able to navigate an openly racist, hateful system and society designed to first enslave us and subsequently see us fail is the strength of the Black family and the support that grew from that strength. Very early on, our government realized the strength of the Black family. They saw it was more than a word; it was a force. Its strength would yield tremendous socioeconomic, societal, and political opportunities that were, from the start, solely intended for white Americans and no one else.

If Black unity persisted, white power would dwindle, so they had to do something—everything—to weaken, separate, and break apart the pillar that would prove to be the foundation of our success. The strategies to destroy the Black family were far-reaching.

Despite the reasoning, there is a tendency to blame Black women for raising children alone. Parenthood in this country is difficult. Single-parenthood is extremely difficult. Single-parenthood for Black women often feels impossible. Funding for schools is determined by zip code, which means the most affluent communities can provide the best education. Most Black people do not live in the most affluent communities. Education often correlates with crime rates. Poverty begets misery, which speaks to mental health. Mental health care is rare in Black communities, but food desserts and liquor stores are commonplace. They say money doesn't buy happiness, but it sure does solve a lot of problems that cause unhappiness. Government programs that were rolled out as means to help struggling families aren't truly for the family unit at all.

In order to qualify for many of these programs, like SNAP, for example, a three-person family cannot have a higher income than $29,940 a year. That's a much easier metric to meet with only one income in the home. Couple the promise of government income with the already-deteriorating family unit in the wake of the War on Drugs of the 1980s and 1990s, and you get a fracture that's been difficult to overcome.

The War on Drugs was especially successful in the breakdown of the Black family. Watching loved ones fall victim to crack-cocaine and end up locked up, strung out, or dead sparked severe trauma, causing us to implode and hate each other and ourselves, destroying ourselves from within. I believe we eventually reached a place of contentment or complacency, where we were no longer willing to sacrifice our own stability for another family or even a family member. Achievement became a "white" thing, so if someone strove for success in a way others didn't understand, they'd become the black sheep, ridiculed and criticized for their intentions.

This encouraged some to implode under the pressure of losing family because they chose to pursue their dreams, while others saw their purpose and growth hindered by lack of support. Those who were able to push past these pressures and attain success often debranched from their family trees, worried they'd be used by family, become a crutch for family, or lose their success trying to support everybody who felt entitled to a portion of it. All of this hindered much of the political and social power we could have, as a people, achieved by now. For these reasons, it's important to discuss generational curses and past animosity. If we are going to advance as a community, which is within our grasp to do, we must come together, communicate, exercise our strengths, and bridge generational gaps. Only then can we share the knowledge to take care of what's ours.

There was a time when an ancestor would secure a piece of property in hopes of passing it down. At some point, the value of that was lost, and it became commonplace for someone down the line to acquire the property, fail to see its true value, and let it go. This hurts us because ownership is what helps us advance most quickly as a community. It also hurts us because it diminishes what someone who planned for later financial security hoped the family would accomplish.

Family isn't just about a sense of belonging; it's also where you build economic legacies. This is one reason, among many, why the Transatlantic Slave Trade had long-lasting negative implications on the financial health of the Black American family. The inability to own land put a dent in the ability to acquire generational wealth. The lack of finances coupled with the lack of knowledge of how to build wealth put Black people far behind our white counterparts. While they were generations deep in acquisition, we were just learning the basics. On paper, the slave trade has been over for 215 years, but the consequences still provide hurdles in every aspect of Black American life.

In addition to financial challenges, slavery set a precedent for excessive work that doesn't align with appropriate compensation, sparked a plethora of mental health issues that seem to only just now be getting the attention they deserve, and set the stage for the fracture of the Black family.

Despite what has become commonplace, there is strong evidence that the most stable living arrangement for the health and growth of children is a healthy, two-parent household. It is always possible for people to thrive outside the norm or break through the concrete and bloom through difficult situations. I'm a prime example. However, when it comes to providing the most fertile environment for children to learn, dream, and work towards self-actualization, the numbers are clear. According to the Institute for Family Studies, "Data from the NLSY97 indicate young adults from intact families are almost twice as likely to graduate from college than their peers who grew up with single parents, and approximately 1.5 times more likely to have a college degree compared to peers in stepfamilies.

After controlling for maternal education, as well as young adults' gender, age, and AFQT scores, we find the odds of Black young adults getting a college degree are almost 70% higher if they were raised by their own two parents." Additionally, "Young Black adults in non-intact homes have about two times the odds of having ever been incarcerated compared to their peers in intact homes"[1] Why is this? Several reasons.

Consider the amount of support children receive from having two well-adjusted adults in the home. It's true that just because there are two doesn't mean they're both well-adjusted, but it's also true that single-parent households usually have the stressors of less income, less time to spend with children, and higher stress stemming from the pressure of the custodial parent trying to make it on their own.

The numbers also show that over the years, marriage is becoming less and less of a staple in the Black community. Consider the statistics from ChildTrends that state, "From 1987 to 2017, the rates of cohabitation among Black women ages 19 to 44 increased from 36 percent to 62 percent, a rate similar to that seen among women from other racial groups. The percentage of Black women ever married, however, is lower than those who have cohabitated, at 37 percent."[2] This issue has been a topic of discussion in various circles for decades. When considering the reasons for this phenomenon, theories such as the wage

---

1. "Bridging the Data Gap for Marriage and Family Research: Potential Opportunities within the NLSY97."
2. "Family, Economic, and Geographic Characteristics of Black Families with Children - Child Trends."

disparities between Black men and women or so many Black men being incarcerated that it lessens the options in the pool of potential partners inevitably top the list of reasons. That means a disproportionate number of Black children are growing up in single-parent households, with women serving as the custodial parent almost all the time. What does this mean for the children? According to ChildTrends, "Sixty-four percent of Black children live in single-parent families, which may include single parents living with an unmarried partner or with another family."[3]

It isn't that children who live in single-parent homes aren't getting love, support, or encouragement. Single parents often do the best they can with what they have, and we all know someone who grew up in like households and went on to do well for themselves. We celebrate them and their parents for their success. However, before success comes, there is a tremendous amount of struggle. As with most things, it comes down to the money. According to IFS, "Homes headed by single parents are about 3.5 times more likely to be living in poverty compared to Black children living with two parents in a first marriage." Whether we like it or not, the makeup of the family is a reliable determinant of the future success of our youth.

When I say family, I'm not solely referring to people we share a bloodline with; I'm speaking of loyalty. Family is who's there with and for you during tough times and celebratory experiences. It includes the people in our lives who are committed to loving and supporting us unconditionally with agape love, those we're bound to through shared struggle. While it would be easy for everyone if the individuals we're born into a unit with were automatically family (as some believe is the case), that isn't always true. There are many dangers in this assumption, one being that in the pursuit of acceptance, we can go looking for family in the wrong places.

---

3. Ibid.

We are relational beings. Everyone is looking for a place to belong. Sometimes, the desire to belong can take us to a place of detriment. If we don't show our young ones love and understanding, the streets and the world will show them something that looks like love and understanding. If we choose to criticize and judge the younger generation instead of meshing the wisdom of age with their knowledge, skill, and zeal, they'll stop listening and go where someone will hear them. and then, when they're dead or in jail, we'll criticize them instead of looking to see where we failed them.

There isn't one person on the planet who doesn't desire family. This desire is well-fulfilled if there are people around to provide that need in a healthy way. However, if a person is ostracized enough by those who are supposed to accept them, they'll go wherever feels like home. It's our responsibility to make it a priority to feel like home and to be careful who we refer to as family. Those who only contribute negativity or care about us when it's good for them aren't family.

When we exhibit healthy behavior and hold those around us to the same standard, we get to see the true essence of the Black family: flavor, power, uniqueness, talent. Our example serves as an example for everyone around us. When you look around, you see evidence of the Black experience everywhere—in music, television, literature, theater, sports, fashion, education, cuisine—there's nowhere you can look and not see the influence. When we see Black people in stable social environments, we get the opportunity to see what we could achieve if we work to put the statistics in reverse and provide solid foundations for our mental, physical, emotional, and intellectual health to thrive. Once we crack that code, we will become unstoppable.

Strategies to Strengthen Black Families in the Hood

1. Acknowledge and unpack the generations worth of trauma that may be currently negatively impacting the family.

2. Invest more time into family outings and revive family reunions. Many families sadly no longer hold family reunions, which I believe are an essential tool for building up the Black family.

3. Utilize counseling and therapy.

4. Be open to talking about difficult things – like mistakes – and all kinds of feelings, including anger, joy, frustration, fear, and anxiety.

5. Acknowledge each others' differences, talents, and abilities, and use each others' strengths. We must also rid ourselves of the crabs in a barrel mentality.

Inspiration

The late Nipsey Hussle once stated, "The best thing you can do for a person is to inspire them. That's the best currency you can offer: inspiration. So, when a person can rely on you for that, that empowers them in every realm of their life—being inspired. It empowers them in their relationships, in their business, in their art, and in their creativity. It empowers them because, without inspiration, you're dry."

Inspiration is a spark that moves your heart and then puts the gears of your mind in motion. It unlocks the mind to new possibilities by allowing us to push past our ordinary experiences and limitations and see ourselves in spaces we hadn't previously imagined. Inspiration is the fuel that propels us towards what others thought impossible, to break stereotypes, and to take control of our narrative and our future. Considering that inspiration wields such power, how important do you find it to be while journeying the road towards your own definition of success? I asked several individuals this question. Here are their responses:

> *"Inspiration is what keeps me moving on the journey that God has planned out for me. As I go through life and all of the struggles it brings, just knowing the fact that people from my hometown of Flint look up to me and keep telling me that I have inspired them in so many ways and to go do things they would never do pushes me to succeed in my plans and to never give up on what I need to do."*
>
> –Phillip Blackamore, Ferris State Student, Flint, MI Native

"Inspiration is key. The road gets dark, and it gets cold. Inspiration houses the light you need to accept motivation in order to move forward."

–Damedot, Hip-Hop Artist, Detroit, MI Native.

"I think inspiration is essential as you work to achieve your goals. Maya Angelou's poem "Still I Rise" has always inspired me to keep moving forward. She ends the poem with the following words, "Bringing the gifts that my ancestors gave; I am the dream and the hope of the slave." Maya Angelou's words remind me of how far Black people have come in the United States. Knowing that my ancestors didn't give up when others put every obstacle they could imagine in Black people's way makes me feel obligated to keep trying. I guess knowing that "I am the dream and the hope of the slave" is my inspiration."

–Angela K Guy-Lee, Ph.D., Adjunct Professor, Ferris State University

Most, if not all, of those who've found success would say inspiration was a critical component along their journey. Unfortunately, the sad reality is that many young people and adults across the nation, specifically those living in urban communities, lack the opportunity to see people who look like them and live where they live in positions of achievement or notability. While there are countless examples of Black success on television, for some people, the lives they see on television are too far a climb from their situations, nothing more than fiction. For others, it's just the spark they need.

For some, they need an example that's close enough to touch. Another reason is the mentality of many individuals who declare, "I'm just trying to make it out the hood!" If they're *just* trying to make it out the hood, once they matriculate through life and become doctors, lawyers, or entrepreneurs, or find themselves in other gainful avenues of employment, they leave the hood and never return. When this happens, our youth are robbed of the opportunity to see and get to know someone they can relate to who started off just like they did. This mentality deprives the youth of seeing positive role models within the community, widening the distance between their current reality and their possible future. However, if it's too much of a lift to get successful people to return to the hood, all is not lost; this is the power of education.

Education begets inspiration. Think for a moment about the difference it could have made in children's lives to have learned about Katherine Johnson, who calculated the trajectory of Apollo 11 to the moon; Ron Stallworth, the first Black graduate of the Colorado Springs Police Cadet

Program who infiltrated the KKK;[4] Bass Reeves, the Deputy US Marshal who brought in more than 3000 outlaws to tame lawless territory;[5] Esther Jones, the Vaudeville performer who inspired the cartoon character, "Betty Boop;" and other notable Black figures whom most of us knew nothing of until recently!

Because of the failure to teach past generations of young Black children about our pioneers, generations worth of potential and equity within the Black community and within the hood were strategically erased by our country's school system and government. Although the system is partly to blame, another part of the blame is on us who failed to provide inspiration to those who are from where we're from. Specifically, I'm referring to those who:

1. Are from the hood.

2. Achieved what they have defined as success.

3. Left the hood once achieving that success.

---

4. Miller, "BlacKKKlansman: The True Story of How Ron Stallworth Infiltrated the K.K.K."

5. "Old West Lawmen."

4. Have not poured back into the hood through either finances or mentorship.

Why wouldn't people return to their roots and offer a hand up to those coming behind them? The reality is many people experienced deep hurt when they were there and have no desire to go back to a place that hurt them. However, the most thorough healing can take place when you go back to the place that hurt you, and when you go back, make it your mission to help mold the hood into what you wished it could have been for you when you were growing up. Shape it in a way that it loses the power to hurt another being the way it hurt you. Another reason people leave and refuse to come back is because of the immense hatred within the hood. Sadly, I can't blame them.

Too many times, I have heard of people going back to their respective neighborhoods upon graduating only to be killed by someone in that same hood months, or even weeks, later. Hate is a strong sentiment, but love is stronger. Hate is a lack of love, therefore, the hood needs love. Love grows where there is inspiration, when there is something to look forward to, and when people believe there is a future self to work towards. Your power lies in your ability to inspire. So many young people in the hood need to see you there!

There are many outstanding examples of people who give of themselves to provide inspiration to the youth of underprivileged communities. Some of them you might know, most of their names you'll never know. We're all aware of athletes, actors, musicians, politicians, business moguls, and others in a variety of other capacities who have made it financially. Especially around the holidays, these stories are spread far and wide. But even when there is no press or name recognition, people are still doing the work.

Tamar Manasseh of Chicago, Founder and President of Mothers Against Senseless Killings, or MASK, saw the epidemic of gun violence in her city destroy a new family each day. She's the mother of two teenagers and decided if something would happen, she'd have to do it. From the first day of summer break to Labor Day, MASK goes onto blocks, cooks dinner daily, and shows love and a presence to the community, providing a safe space for children to play. "If we bring love to those corners, nothing else can exist there. Nothing is stronger than love; not even bullets. In the end, this is not just about stopping violence, it's about building community," says Manasseh.

In the two years after MASK was founded, there wasn't one shooting on one of the worst blocks on the southside of Chicago. Manasseh believed that since gun violence was everywhere, MASK needed to be everywhere, too. At the time of the Steve Harvey Show broadcast where she was named a "Harvey's Hero," the organization had made connections with Staten Island, New York and Evansville, Indiana and were working on connections in Los Angeles, Las Vegas, Miami, Memphis, and wherever else people were willing to carry on the program. One of her teammates had a daughter who was killed by gun violence, and she used that pain as inspiration to prevent other mothers from suffering the same pain she has.[6]

In a small town in Mississippi, when Mississippi was #50 in education and communities were feeling the drain in every way, a citizen of a small town, Roy Acker, started an organization called Community of Christians Helping Youth, or C.C.H.Y. What started off as a local tutoring service in the 1990s is still alive today, providing tutoring and philanthropic opportunities for Black students in the town of Picayune, MS. Alumni of the program, both tutors and tutees alike, have gone on to graduate, attain rank in the military, travel the world, and establish various notable careers.

When you provide inspiration, you don't have to do it alone. Others will see the vision and get on board. It only takes one brave soul to start. One of the most beautiful things about inspiration is that it's

---

6. Steve TV Show, "#RealGood: Fighting Gun Violence with Love | STEVE HARVEY."

contagious. One person getting out of their comfort zone empowers others to do the same, like using the flame of a candle to light the wick of others.

There is a reason organizations pay thousands of dollars for inspirational speakers. We want to feel something that touches our most human instinct to make a difference. American psychologist Abraham Maslow developed what we know as "Maslow's Hierarchy of Needs," a pyramid that explains human motivation. According to his theory, you cannot meet a need until the one below it has been met. From the bottom to the top, the needs are:

- Physiological needs: air, water, food, clothing, shelter

- Safety needs: personal security, employment, resources, health, property

- Love and belonging: friendship, intimacy, family, connection

- Esteem: respect, self-esteem, status, recognition, strength, freedom

- Self-actualization: desire to become the most you can be

It's hard for people to dream about their highest selves when they're struggling to figure out where their next meal is coming from. Often, it takes someone else to show them there is something real beyond the blinding darkness of pain. Remember, hard does not mean impossible. That's why any time is a good time to provide inspiration for someone. Additionally, if you do go into the hood to provide inspiration, go with something tangible that can help your audience in a real way. If you can provide food, do it. If you can provide water to a community that needs it, do it. If you can provide jobs, do it. If you can provide any resources, do it, because that helps to open the path to the rest of the hierarchy. If you are in a place of love, esteem, and self-actualization, you have more to give than you might think.

Strategies to Bring Inspiration into the Hood

1. Be an example. Live in such a way that the life you live will speak for itself.

2. Be caring. "People don't care about how much you know until they know how much you care." –Lewis Howes

3. Be encouraging. Remember, we all have bad days. Knowing this, strive to be an individual who encourages the people around them to keep pushing. Help people discover the best within themselves.

4. Educate. Keep your brain refreshed by continuously feeding it with knowledge, and surround yourself with people who contribute to your personal growth. Stay informed about what's going on in your community and the world. Lastly, and most importantly, take that information and pour it into the next generation.

5. Be open. Be as willing to share your failures as you are to share your successes. Our young people need to know that it is okay to fail, and failure is not the end! We've all lost at some point in our lives, and we should utilize those failures to help those we encounter daily to realize they can bounce back from any setback in life.

6. Communicate. To truly inspire others, you must learn to communicate with them on their level. Simply meet people where they are and articulate to them understandably and effectively. Humility is key in this aspect. No one wants to be talked at or to engage in conversations with someone whose speech feels condescending. Remember, people want a guide by their side, not a sage on the stage.

7. Love genuinely. Love has the power to keep us feeling hopeful and brighten our darkest days. Pour out that love. Don't do this for the media, for accolades, or to make yourself look good; do it because it's the right thing to do.

Education

One definition of education is *the result produced by instruction, training, or study.*[7] It's the acquisition of knowledge or skills, but I believe it's more than that.

Education is the radical liberation of one's mind, body, and soul. It's the gift of enlightenment and empowerment, the North Star that helps guide us into our purpose. It can come from a variety of sources, and if we train ourselves to be students of the endless lessons that are evolving around us each day, it can come from anywhere.

As an anti-racist practitioner in higher education, my approach to education acknowledges our position in the web of power, privilege, and oppression that has been embedded within the framework of our country's educational system. When students enter my classrooms, they can expect to learn about social justice through lectures, dialogue, readings, and experiential exercises that demonstrate the social construction of various social identities and how those constructs survive through thought processes, policies, and practices. Through this approach, I seek to move beyond merely recognizing the social constructions of institutions, but to make connections regarding how those institutions impact citizens' lives either through privilege or oppression.

---

7. "Education Definition & Meaning | Dictionary.Com."

It is becoming more commonplace for those in political power to attempt to restrict teaching, both at the K-12 and university levels, pertaining to the raw history of how our country came to be. Although many seem taken aback by these attempts, they are not new. Historically, education has been gate kept in many ways, chief among them being the quality of education a student receives based on their zip code. It is true that since we pay taxes with the expectation (and sometimes, unfounded hope) of those funds going toward quality education for our youth, it is not only the system who is responsible for filling the intellectual gap for our youth.

We, as a community, are equally responsible, especially when it comes to our own history, and even more especially if we want that history expelled through a socially just framework. There is so much our schools didn't teach us, therefore, we have to participate in a great deal of learning, unlearning, and relearning if we are to be well-informed participants in society. Furthermore, we cannot allow a lack of quality and/or authentic education from our schools to be an excuse for ignorance.

We can only expect the system to be what it is, therefore, we must be willing to teach ourselves and explore higher learning on our own. As far as the community is concerned, it's our responsibility to bridge generational gaps, learn from everyone around us, and proudly embrace our history, present, and future. Over the years, we have had shining examples of proponents of autodidactic education, as W.E.B. DuBois, James Baldwin, and Malcolm X wholeheartedly believed in the power of educating oneself. When it comes to foundational understanding of the topic, their speeches and writings are priceless.

From a general perspective, one may say the purpose of formal education is to pour into an individual to empower them to better navigate life and contribute to society once they become tax-paying citizens, a goal that is closely tied to a capitalistic economic perspective. Historically, it appears that institutional learning on American soil has provided education that is just quality enough to enable the historically privileged to continue to amass wealth and power, but provide just enough education in the hood to allow marginalized individuals to acquire just enough skills to barely get by, sacrificing their bodies and purpose to make someone else rich while still attempting to wriggle out from under the thumb of oppression.

From a social justice and anti-racist lens, I believe the purpose of education is to help eradicate the issues affecting our lives in a negative way. Done right, education is the catalyst that equips the current and coming generations of change agents. Once you have it, no one can take it away. Once you have it, it is paramount that you pass it on to someone else. However, systems are effective, especially those that are the reason behind this topic of conversation still existing in the first place. So, the natural question is: *How does one go about effectively educating themselves?*

There is no one empirical pathway of education. For a period of time, the belief was that a person had to do well through grade school and go to college to become successful. If they wanted to become very successful, they needed to pursue postgraduate studies. That's simply no longer the case. The abundance of opportunities to propel one towards success today includes trade school, military, entrepreneurship, apprenticeships, online studies, and so much more, including community college. While some may look down at community college, they are excellent institutions to begin a college education.

They save students money and help propel them towards what is coming next. I'm a proud community college alum who started my journey homeless and now holds degrees and certificates from Henry Ford College, Ferris State, University of Michigan, and Harvard, and I'm not done yet. If entrepreneurship tugs at your heart and mind, look into social entrepreneurship and seek out mentors. If you want to be surrounded by floods of students and professors who look like you and are striving towards similar goals, consider an HBCU. These institutions have rich heritages that were created and maintained from the desire of Black people to pursue an education but who weren't allowed because of racist laws and ideals. They continue to thrive and equip students to be competitive in the workforce.

The key is not a particular stringent path; the key is to develop yourself into a forever student and never stop learning. The goal is not to acquire knowledge and flaunt it in front of others. If you're the smartest person in the room, go find another room where you can continue to grow.

We live in the Age of Information, and sometimes it's hard to know which sources are reliable. One route towards a solid self-education is to begin with notable figures in the Black community, like Huey P. Newton, Angela Davis, Katherine Johnson, James Baldwin, W.E.B. DuBois, Fred Hampton, and Malcolm X. Read up thoroughly on stories and figures the history books glossed over or whitewashed, like Dr. Martin Luther King Jr. Seek out primary sources and comb through them so you know for yourself exactly what these figures stood for and how they transformed over time. Take advantage of the various resources that dive deeply into our history, and always fact check.

When students learn about Black history in a standard American classroom, there are a handful of topics teachers are guaranteed to cover. They'll start with the Transatlantic Slave Trade, which implies that Black history began with slavery. Very rarely will you find a classroom that discusses what Africans were doing before slavery. Using such a horrific event that spanned over so many years as a launching pad to teach our history creates a paradigm that Black people were not doing much before the boats showed up. When you self-educate, dig deeper. Learn about Mansa Musa. Learn about the various kingdoms through the continent of Africa, learn where math originated, and learn about hubs of culture and education like Timbuktu.

After the slave trade, students will learn about Abraham Lincoln and how he ended slavery. What they will not learn is Lincoln's true beliefs about Black people. They will not read the Lincoln-Douglass debates or learn about how Lincoln never intended for Black people to be equal to whites in America. They will not learn that he made decisions towards ending slavery for political reasons. They'll learn about the Civil War, and depending on where they are, some teachers will teach the war was about slavery, and others will argue it was about states' rights, but not states' rights to own slaves.

Students in Advanced Placement classes will learn about the Reconstruction Era, the time after the Civil War when the powers that be attempted to rework American society to include its new Black citizens. They might even learn about how slave owners were awarded land while former slaves received no reparations. They'll learn about sharecroppers. Some teachers will say Reconstruction succeeded; others will say it failed.

Then they'll skip over to the Civil Rights Movement, where they may learn about Emmitt Till's brutal murder by white men in Mississippi after Carolyn Bryant claimed the teenage boy made a pass at her. They may or may not learn that those men were never convicted, or that Carolyn Bryant, who died at 89, never faced consequences for her lie. They'll learn about Rosa Parks refusing to sit on the back on the bus, and of course, they'll learn about Dr. Martin Luther King, Jr. They will not learn that he was the most hated man in America while he exercised his part of the movement. They'll learn about his murder, and many students will walk away believing MLK ended racism.

After that, students might learn about Barack Obama being the first Black president, and that is essentially where it all ends. George Washington Carver might make an appearance in a few lesson plans, but essentially, Black history will fit on five or fewer pages of a textbook, and the horrors will be reduced to something that's a thing of the past. In fact, a 2015 study by the National Museum of African American History and Culture and Oberg Research found, "on average, only 8%

or 9% of history class time in US schools is devoted to Black history."[8] However, when you start to dig for yourself, you'll uncover a variety of truths that likely will never make their way into a classroom:

- One in four cowboys was Black.

- Vaccinations came from the mind of an enslaved African named Onesimus, a practice they'd been exercising in Africa for centuries.

- HBCUs were places of refuge for persecuted Jews during World War II.

- Before Rosa Parks refused to give up her seat on a bus, Claudette Colvin did the same thing. She ended up being a catalyst to overturn segregation laws in Alabama.

These facts don't even scratch the surface. The history of Black people in this country could fill volumes of encyclopedias. While it's impossible to know all of it, it's possible, and even expected, to seek and pursue this knowledge. If we don't know where we came from, we can't truly know who we are.

When it comes to learning about our history in the classroom, we are not powerless. Students have more power than they might realize. If they want a Black history elective, they can approach the school board in their district and ask if such a class can be added to the list of options for the next year or semester. If the board says yes, the students will need to get a certain number of signatures on a petition and get a teacher to agree to teach the class. If they meet these requirements, they can have the class. One thing we should always remember is that this country claims to be a democracy. That means the populace gets to make many of the decisions. The pen is mightier than the sword, so it's important to

---

8. Colarossi, "African American History You Probably Weren't Taught in School."

know what the laws and regulations say and figure out an appropriate strategy to get what you want.

Education is the way out of oppression, and today, in this Age of Information, knowledge is readily available. Wherever there is an internet connection and a screen or audio, there is an opportunity for education. Wherever there is a listening ear and a mind that knows how to engage in logic, there is an opportunity for education. If we choose not to take advantage of these resources and educate ourselves, we will repeat the detriments in our history. If we don't choose education, we are doomed to fail.

Think about the talent in the hood, talent of all kinds. There are great scientific minds, culinary artists, visual artists, musicians, athletes, mechanics—any skillset a person can imagine, you can find it among our people. Once we pair that talent and creativity with a quality education, there is nothing we cannot accomplish. The descendants of those who've tried to keep us from realizing our potential and who desire to carry on the heritage of their ancestors know this, which is why they do all they can to limit our educational attainment. However, the power is in our hands.

Strategies for Promoting Education in the Hood

1. Create a mentorship program.

2. Create a tutoring program.

3. Volunteer where the kids are and teach them what they need to know. Vow to listen twice as much as you talk.

4. Expose the youth to the arts.

5. Celebrate MLK Day, Juneteenth, and Kwanzaa as a community.

6. Hold events for those who've made it out the hood to come back and share their knowledge with the youth.

7. Start a community garden.

Antiracism

Anyone who would make the argument that we live in a post-racial society hasn't been paying attention. The U.S.A. is just as guilty today as it's always been when it comes to perpetuating racist ideals and systems. The reckoning our country has experienced since the murder of Trayvon Martin, which was the switch point for the Black Lives Matter movement, has put racism in America under a microscope. Since then, we've watched many high-profile murders of Black men and women serve as reminders that racism is alive and well, and it's up to our society to eradicate it. This is where antiracism comes into play.

The term "antiracist" was made popular by Ibram X. Kendi, author of *Stamped from the Beginning*, a commentary on racism in America throughout the years and how it's affected every area of life as we know it. His teachings and philosophies boldly and honestly shed light on the fact that it is not good enough for one to simply declare they are not racist, but it is essential to be antiracist. Antiracism is active. It transforms thoughts and sentiments into actions and forces us to address the issue of race head on instead of passively declaring one doesn't have anything against anybody or one doesn't see color.

Antiracism results from a conscious decision to make frequent, consistent, equitable choices on a daily basis that require ongoing self-awareness and reflection as we move through life. When we are not actively antiracist, we subconsciously uphold aspects of white supremacy, white-dominant culture, and unequal institutions in society. Being racist or antiracist isn't about who you are; it's about what you do.

The year 2020 forced everyone to consider where they stand in the fight for equality. Protests all around the world exploded as we watched Derick Chauvin choke the life out of George Floyd on an endless loop for days that became weeks. The murders of Ahmad Arbury and Breonna Taylor added fuel to the fire, and before we knew it, everyone cared about the state of Black lives in America. It seemed that everyone was making a commitment to be better and to do better, although many doubted the wave would last much longer than the moment.

But for the moment, corporations, educational institutions, sports teams, and all kinds of other organizations were ready to dismantle their problematic ways of thinking and do the work to make society better for minorities. Of course, this wasn't everyone, but the sentiment was alive the world over. Companies and organizations created DEI departments, schools implemented curriculum to teach the things that haven't historically been taught in classrooms about Black history, present, and past, and Black people informed and reminded those seeking knowledge that it wasn't necessarily our responsibility to educate them. It was a rare time in the country and the world.

What we saw more blatantly than anything at this time was the difference between those who truly cared to make a difference and those who didn't care to be the difference.

Those who vowed to be antiracist made a commitment to pivot from a passive belief system about how society functions for people of color to an active one of learning the ugly truth about history, teaching their children about the reality of people who don't look like them, and refusing to allow racist speech or behavior to take place unchecked in their presence. This is important because of the very real dangers marginalized groups face every day. For instance, a phone call to the police for a white person might mean help is on the way, but for a Black person, it could very well mean injury or death.

The healthcare system could mean a healthy start for a white mother and her baby, but it might mean another addition to the maternal mortality rate for a Black mother and child of the same socioeconomic status. It might mean SPED inclusion for a Black student where it would mean gifted placement for a white one. It means animalistic, thuggish ways for Black people where it means mental illness for white people. The differences are endless and make it clear that we function in two separate realities, and the only way to do anything about it is to first be able to see it. For those ready to not only see it, but to face it, the resources are vast.

The explosion of books, courses, webinars, podcasts, websites, town halls, and other means of education and communication was like Mt. Vesuvius. It was felt far and wide and affected everyone who knew about it. One of the most deeply felt changes was the jolt of electricity that shot through the field of Diversity, Equity, and Inclusion.

Let's start with the classroom. A study of six focus groups composed of parents/guardians of color at schools across three Midwestern school districts concluded that families of ACE-impacted students of color (those impacted by adverse childhood experiences) experienced racism from the school community, which discouraged engagement and interfered with relationships between family and school staff. Additionally, "Parents highlighted feeling excluded from decisions related to their child's education and that their voices were not heard or understood.

Participants discussed the need for schools to consider how family obstacles (such as mental health and trauma) may prevent families from engaging with staff, and they recommended structural changes, such as antiracism training for educators."[9]

---

9. Piper et al., "The Importance of Anti-Racism in Trauma-Informed Family Engagement."

This is the work that encourages positive change. We know education is the ticket to success, but if students feel trapped in a web of discrimination within the walls of their school, they will suffer the consequences both intellectually and emotionally. This type of effort is necessary in the classroom as well as life well beyond the classroom.

DEI is now a department in businesses all across the country, both officially and unofficially. The departments exist to ensure fair and equitable practices in hiring, employee experience, and customer experience. While there were absolutely organizations that did this just for show, once the wave receded, there were many that held on to their commitment to equity. While this looks like a great thing, we must remember that DEI is hard work, and we need to support those who are doing the hard work on this level day in and day out.

It wasn't only corporations who made such commitments. Of course, people did the same on an individual level. These people are what's referred to as allies, or "those who make the commitment and effort to recognize their privilege (based on gender, class, race, sexual identity, etc.) and work in solidarity with oppressed groups in the struggle for justice."[10] Allies understand that it is in their own best interest to end all forms of oppression, even those from which they may benefit in concrete ways. True allies are those who are willing to sacrifice their own beneficial power and privilege for the common good. A person can certainly wake up one morning and declare they want to be an ally, but becoming a true ally doesn't happen overnight. It is a process of dismantling problematic beliefs and replacing them with the truth. The University of Pittsburgh has a robust set of recommendations for those looking to participate in antiracism in this capacity:

There is no prescriptive method to becoming an ally, but there are steps that everyone must follow to become better informed. The University

---

10. "The AAJ Glossary - Anti-Racism and Allyship 7 Day Journey."

of Pittsburgh has a clear list of the Dos and Don'ts of allyship that is worth taking the time to explore:

1. ***Who are you?*** *Look inward and create an identity map that lists your place in society. Think about your race, gender, ethnicity, family roles, professional roles, and religious affiliations. Understanding how you've reached your worldview is important to understanding your relationship to other people, ideas, and events.*

2. ***Educate yourself!*** *Begin thinking about your own identity map and challenge yourself to learn more about the groups, cultures, and identities that you do not identify with. Have you experienced privilege in a way that those in other groups have not? It is only through learning about others that you can stand with them and advocate for them, using your own power and privilege in ways that marginalized voices cannot.*

3. ***Use your new found skills.*** *Recognizing the differences in power and privilege among social groups is only the first step. Learn how to communicate your thoughts about privilege, power, and oppression. It may be scary at first, so look for a way to practice these skills in safe environments.*

4. ***Take action.*** *Being an ally means more than just knowing the right things to say. Get out in the community and talk to others about the struggle marginalized groups go through.*[11]

One of the most important things for an ally to remember is who the effort is about. It's human nature to try to relate when we see someone going through a hard time, but allyship is 100% about turning the attention to the marginalized group you're supporting. Over and over again, Black people hear about reverse racism from white people and all the ways they've been discriminated against because of the color

---

11. "Guides: Anti-Black Racism: History, Ideology, and Resistance - Oakland Campus: Ally to Accomplice."

of their skin. Meanwhile, those complaining about reverse racism fail to recognize that the systems that make the country and the world go around were built for white people, specifically white men with money. White women are the second group who have immediately benefitted the most from those systems because of their proximity to white men. Everyone else is on the margins. Some might make the argument that white people can experience racism.

When it comes to prejudice, yes, white people can be on the receiving end. But when it comes to racist systems and institutions on which society is built, since those systems were created by and for white people, they cannot, by definition, experience racism. This is a privilege they hold, and used correctly by allies, that very privilege can be a tool to move the needle from a racist society to one of equity.

That being said, efforts towards an equitable society have been ongoing since the beginning of time. Yet, the efforts of the Quakers, John Brown, Freedom Fighters, MLK, Malcolm X, the Black Panthers, the BLM movement, all of those not listed, and all the efforts that are ongoing haven't been enough to eradicate racism. Why? There are many reasons.

- Humans are, by nature, prone to comparison. Once people figured out (during the Spanish Inquisition) that racism was an effective way to rank and overpower the people around them, it stuck and became one of the most effective tools of supremacy of any kind.

- Racists breed racists. No one is born racist; people are taught to be that way. While many people who grow up hating others because of their origins find it within themselves to turn away from their beliefs, just as many others don't. As long as there are racists, there will likely always be racists.

- Racism benefits people. Without it, those who currently hold privilege because of it wouldn't hold power anymore, and everyone isn't willing to give up that power.

- It would take the dismantling and rebuilding of many systems to eradicate systemic racism, and the powers that be do all they can to keep that from happening. We are not powerless against the powers that be, but we haven't yet figured out how to overpower them.

To eradicate racism, it would take those with pure intentions in mass numbers infiltrating the system and changing it from within. And while that would be difficult, it would be even more difficult to change the hearts and minds of those who believe one race is superior to another or all others. As difficult as it is to change laws and systems, it's even more difficult to change attitudes and mindsets. And yet, do I believe racism will ever die? Yes, I believe it is possible, but it would take all communities coming together as a collective to bring such a sick and powerful force to an end. Additionally, it would take that same effort to keep it from rising up again and to keep another force just as sinister from taking its place.

Strategies to Implement Antiracism for the Benefit of the Hood

1. We must stop lying to society and ourselves and move on from the notion that we can "fix the system." I would argue that the system that upholds racism within the framework of our nation has never been broken to begin with. Instead, it is working exactly the way it was intended to. Therefore, we must move closer towards the notion of dismantling, eradicating, and rebuilding the frameworks of our nation's soul and society as a whole.

2. We must continue our fight for equitable reparations, as Black people are the only people who have not received much-owed reparations from the United States government for the genocide we've experienced. What happened to our promise of 40 acres and a mule?

3. This nation, especially Black men, must take a stand to protect, love, respect, and fight for and with our Black women, as Black women are the true backbone of our nation. **This is non-negotiable.**

4. We must push for more antiracist legislation, both locally, state-wide, and federally, and incorporate antiracism in every aspect of our lives.

Unity

Poet and author Ryunosuke Satoro once stated, "Individually, we are one drop. Together, we are an ocean." The power in that statement speaks volumes. Think of all the times we've seen this sentiment play out. Jordan's legacy would not have been as impactful without Scottie Pippen or Dennis Rodman. Neil Armstrong and Buzz Aldrin wouldn't have made it to the moon on July 20, 1969 if there were no Katherine Johnson. No matter how skilled or athletic, quarterbacks couldn't make it to the Superbowl by relying solely on their own skills.

There would be no activist, author, musician, nor preacher known to the world as Byron D. Brooks had there not been Roscoe and Joesther Corner who, out of sheer love, raised their great-grandson, who was born in prison, as their own son. We were never meant to realize our greatness on our own. If we were, we wouldn't be surrounded by millions of other people. No one is self-made; everybody has had some kind of help from somebody. We only have the knowledge and skillset to do so much. Individually, we are one drop, but together, we're an ocean. Think of all the times you've seen this truth in your own life experiences.

A mentor of mine once asked me, "Do you believe that violence could be ended within the Black community?" My answer was and still is a firm yes. I know it can happen. I know a peaceful existence could be our reality. I also know that we can never attain it through an individualistic approach. To accomplish such a feat would take inward reflection and outward collaboration. To diffuse violence, we would need a strategic plan and tremendous staying power to see it through. Although there are those who try to blame violence on inherent character traits, the sheer amount of systemic, oppressive, and racial constructions deeply rooted within our nation are the leading causes of so much violence within the Black community. If we analyze, address, and dismantle the root cause of said violence while embedding social equity into our community's framework, we can most certainly end the violence. In order to better understand where the volatility stems from, it's important to understand its root causes to draw more complete conclusions.

According to city-journal.org:

> As for group behavior, cultural factors help explain differences in violent-crime levels. African-Americans, for example, have had high violent-crime rates from the late nineteenth century to the present. These patterns derive from their Southern background, where whites had higher rates of violence than whites in other regions. Early Irish and Italian immigrants also had high crime rates until, having moved into the middle class, they found that such violence became patently self-destructive. Thus, a group's history and experience, not biological determinants such as skin color or race, drive violent behaviors.

> As we saw with Irish and Italian immigration to the United States—and will someday see with America's Black and Latino populations—movement up the social ladder to the middle class is associated with sharp declines in violent crime. The reasons for this are easily appreciated. The middle-class person has everything to lose, and little to gain, from interpersonal violence: personal injury, loss of status, and criminal justice sanctions. Plus, the civil legal system provides effective alternatives for dispute resolution that middle-class individuals can afford.

> Now we can better understand why so many offenders are in the low-income bracket. It isn't that poverty causes crime, but

rather that more affluent people avoid violent conflict, in effect, ceding the field to the poor.[12]

Violence accompanies poverty not only among Black Americans, but among other demographics as well. This is why we must destroy the myth of Black-on-Black crime. The term first came on the scene in 1979 in Ebony magazine and then again in Black Enterprise magazine the same year, but the idea became popular due to the 1896 book, "The Race Traits and Tendencies of the American Negro," by Frederick L. Hoffman, in which the author claimed that Black people had a "special crime problem."[13] However, the stats tell a different story:

- The Bureau of Justice Statistics' 2019 crime victimization statistics report shows those who commit violent acts tend to commit them against members of the same race as the offender.

- Offenders were white in 62% of violent incidents committed against white victims, Black in 70% of incidents committed against Black victims, and Hispanic in 45% of incidents committed against Hispanic victims, according to the BJS report.[14]

Since violent crimes most often take place within races, why is that Black people are the only ones whose crimes are labeled according to race, suggesting that these crimes happen because of their race? It's because of our racist history.

Since the slave trade, lies and pseudoscience have spread throughout society that Black people have smaller brains, Black people are more like animals than humans, and Black people are naturally violent. The first movie played at the White House, *Birth of a Nation*, perpetuated the lie

---

12. City Journal, "Poverty and Violent Crime Don't Go Hand in Hand | City Journal."

13. Lynn, "'Black-on-Black Crime': A Loaded and Controversial Phrase Often Heard amid Calls for Police Reform."

14. "Violent Victimization by Race or Hispanic Origin, 2008–2021 | Bureau of Justice Statistics."

that Black men, by nature, were rapists. This same film was responsible for the sharp growth of the KKK, a movement that was birthed out of fear that stemmed from lies in the first place. These lies settled into the collective American subconscious, and to undo the misinformation, we must be intentional about undoing its indoctrination, learning the true origins of violence in communities (especially our own), and doing the work to break the chains and make space for healthy operating communities.

The term has been used for decades to further divide us, because the more we can stay divided, the longer it will be before we achieve unity. In fact, many socially constructed ideologies and stereotypes were created to deter us from unifying and executing our true essence and potential, and at times, our people, whether they meant to or not, have participated in it. However, in addition to the need to address the tools of division that stem from the term, we must address and deconstruct the nature of colorism.

Colorism is the practice of discrimination in which those with lighter skin are treated more favorably than those with darker skin. This practice is yet another product of racism in the USA and beyond. It upholds the white standards of beauty and benefits white people in the institutions of oppressions, from media to medicine. Let's take a closer look at how colorism has been used in the United States to divide people of color and later used strategically to become the main deterrent of unity within the hood.

During slavery, those with "fair skin" were assigned domestic tasks, like working inside the slave master's house, while those with darker skin were forced to work out in the fields on much more grueling assignments. Fair-skinned slaves were favored over darker slaves because they were often the products of the master's rape of a slave, hence why they had lighter skin. Moving towards the 19th and 20th centuries, the "paper bag test" became a common hiring practice in our society. It played out like this: if a person's skin tone was the same or lighter than the paper bag, they were granted entrance into the space to be considered for hire. If they were any darker than the paper bag, however, they were not allowed into the workspace or given the opportunity to be considered for hire. Therefore, skin tone was often the most important factor in applying for work as a person of color in the mid-20th century. Light skin was often reported on a resume ahead of any other information or experience.

As far as we'd like to think we've come, this way of thinking has survived many generations and hindered the proper trajectory of growth and unity in the hood. If you are a direct product of the hood, my plea to you is simple: go within the communities you are from and educate our young brothers and sisters on the importance of not judging each other based on the tone or fairness of their skin. While there has been a tremendous upswing of media surrounding positivity around whatever skin tone you may have, old habits die hard, and many people still have a long way to go when it comes to accepting people as they are. It's our responsibility to teach them that the character of their being is more powerful, influential, and meaningful than the amount of melanin in their skin.

Show them how to push past stereotypes created through fallacious perceptions that many have adopted in the hood. To my suburban counterpart, I implore you to reflect on how you may have allowed an individual's skin tone to create an ignorant perception of that person's character in your mind. If you truly aspire to help bring unified growth to Detroit, Chicago, and other cities where minorities and their neighborhoods are often marginalized and lack resources, it is not enough to merely set up shop in our downtown areas for economic gain or to give our cities good PR as if your business were some kind of savior.

None of that means anything if your business is not helping in any way or promoting social growth in the underdeveloped communities surrounding our downtown areas. In fact, I stand firm in the notion that this form of doing business has long been a tool of systemic racism and oppression and has hindered the potential of unity more than it has helped.

Sadly, people in many influential positions see the hood as an opportunity for personal gain with no real intention of helping the people there who need it most. Sadly, politicians have cared more about building up and pouring resources into their cities' downtown areas to attract tourists, helping them line their own pockets, rather than utilizing those resources or, at the very least, putting forth the same energy to provide the hood with the same opportunities for growth, entrepreneurial ventures, and economic development. Downtowns everywhere receive millions of dollars for scaling and expansion, but how do those dollars help the underserved?

Meanwhile, neighborhoods such as Brightmoor in Detroit are watching people who don't even live in our city dump their trash in our communities. In fact, many suburban citizens often drive to the hoods of Detroit to illegally dump their trash into our neighborhoods, but they would never dare do such things in their own. Tell me, where is the unity in that?

There is an African proverb that states, "If you want to go quickly, go alone. If you want to go far, go together." We have a long way to go. If we want to see drastic changes in our society before this generation is finished on this earth, we have to go far. The amount of work left to do is too vast to even list. However, there are people in noteworthy positions, sitting around tables to help make it happen. We have the skills, we have the knowledge, and anything we don't have, we have access to. If we come together and mobilize, there isn't much we can't do, but we have to be in it for the long haul. We must survive the frustrations, the heartbreaks, and the letdowns.

We must make unity priority number one. If we do that, and we couple our unity with knowledge and resolve, not only will we go far, but we might even reach our destination more quickly than we thought possible.

Strategies to Promote Unity in the Hood

1. Establish more community enhancing programming.

2. Revive Block Clubs.

3. Establish affinity spaces.

4. Create opportunities for individuals within the hood to form a sense of ownership within their neighborhoods.

5. Establish deliberate dialogues allowing an opportunity for everyone in the community to amplify their voices and have difficult discussions.

6. Teach ourselves and learn about where and how the disconnect within our communities started so we can move forward together.

7. Remember this African Proverb: Ubuntu—I am because WE are!

8. Bridge our generational gaps with love and understanding.

9. Be a listener more than a talker.

Faith

I would be remiss if I didn't address the elephant in the room after expounding on unity in the previous chapter: the theological division caused by racist white evangelists attempting to twist biblical doctrine and Christianity to justify their own racist and hate-filled man-made ideologies and beliefs. Now, I'm no famous theologian, however, it does not take a theologian to recognize how, throughout history, Christianity has been perverted by racism and white supremacy and how that perversion of biblical doctrine has created a racial divide within our nation.

The hypocrisy of white evangelists is truly sad, for not only has it hindered potential social change within society, but over centuries, it has caused many to question the true ethics and validity of Christianity. Going back to the 18th century, we come across an evangelist who also happened to be one of the founders of Methodism and the evangelical movement. His name was George Whitefield.

While Whitefield did condemn the cruelty of slave owners, he simultaneously campaigned for the legalization of slavery in the colony of Georgia. The Reverend Johnathon Edwards, whom history cites as one of America's most important and original philosophical theologians within history, owned many slaves, all while preaching the importance of allowing the evangelization of slaves. Fast forward a few centuries, and we now have evangelists, such as Franklin Graham, comparing Republicans who voted to impeach Trump to the betrayal of Christ!

To make matters worse, Graham made this statement not long after domestic terrorists raided our Capitol Building, resulting in five deaths. I personally find it hard to wrap my head around the fact that any individual can weekly proclaim the gospel of Christ and focus on His liberating victory over death and the cross (which has such a deeply symbolic foreshadowing of the lynching tree, a continuance of which is police brutality in America today), but yet allow their racist ideologies to blind them from using their voices to stand up for social justice.

I must also be honest, though. White evangelists are not the only ones to blame for our country's racial divide and our community's lack of resources and opportunities to rise from an oppressive system built to see us fail. Sadly, within the Black church, many pastors and preachers alike have pimped their calling for their own personal gain. Many have traded liberation theology for prosperity gospel and man-made doctrine that sounds good and could keep their position secure within their church by not ruffling too many feathers.

As it stands, there is a distinct disconnect between the church and the community. This is a result of many churches mirroring more of a glorified country club rather than what the church is intended to represent.

Every Black church should be a catalyst for social change in some form or fashion. While many preachers love to be behind a pulpit, not enough of them are on the front lines when protests erupt. Jesus was no spineless man--he was radical, and it's going to take that same kind of revolutionary spirit to bridge the gaps between race, faith, and justice. While our neighborhoods are hurting spiritually, physically, and emotionally, many churches are sadly focusing more on flashy programs and schemes to bring in funds rather than establishing relationships with their communities. Yet, we question why so many leave or even refuse to bother coming to the church.

Consider the effective role of the Black church during the Civil Rights Movement. Throughout history, churches haven't only provided a space of freedom and safety for Black people, but during the movement, "They hosted mass meetings, were meeting points for rallies and marches, and provided much-needed emotional, physical, moral and spiritual support. These churches gave the community the strength to endure and ultimately succeed in gaining equal human rights for every American regardless of color or creed."[15]

Overall, the church doesn't seem to stand for these values anymore. In fact, so many people have been hurt by the church in so many ways (physically, psychologically, emotionally, and of course, spiritually), that it's hard for them to believe any god would allow such behavior in their very own place of worship and keep people in positions who show no remorse. Today, church attendance is lower than it's ever been in American history, and Black members of the fellowship align with that decline in numbers. Why is that? According to defendernetwork. com, the top five reasons why Black millennials and beyond are leaving the church are:

1. **The church is judgmental and unaccepting.** Why walk into the line of fire on Sunday mornings when you can more effectively fill up your spirit by sleeping in or taking a walk in the park or on the beach?

2. **Black people are choosing traditional spiritual paths.** As we educate ourselves and find how our traditions were demonized during colonization, young Black people are more interested in pursuing religions of the ancestors rather than what they view as the religion of the oppressor.

3. **They see the church as anti-intellectual and closed off to new information.** All too often, asking questions that are difficult to answer is looked down on in church. People

---

15. "Churches Pivotal to the Civil Rights Movement to Visit Today."

of logic are supposed to be satisfied with answers like, "God works in mysterious ways," or "You just have to have faith." The education they're encouraged to pursue doesn't jibe with blind faith. Many times, if a religious leader doesn't know the answer, they berate the person asking instead of humbly admitting they just don't know.

4. **Too many churches are apolitical.** Politics affect every aspect of our lives. If churches are "too heavenly focused to be any earthly good," how is being part of the church helping the congregation get through the struggles of everyday life?

5. **Their peers are missing.** And why is that? Too many churches aren't receptive to change. If young people don't feel at home, why would they go?[16]

Jesus challenged religious authority, spoke truth to power, and was a true agent of change. He wasn't conservative in His ways, nor did He care anything about preserving the status quo. We often talk about living a Christ-like life. It's time for all church leaders to embrace that talk by transforming our air into action! Black churches, whether we want to admit it or not, see the injustices and lack of resources that are hurting the communities in which our buildings reside. However, too many of us pray in private only to then become silent in public when it comes to social justice and ethics issues within our communities. Of course, this is not the case with all churches, but as a young believer, I must say that there are not enough of our churches and leaders on the front lines for social change.

To any pastor, bishop, or priest that may be reading this, allow me to ask you a question on behalf of hoods everywhere: Have you become more fixated on how you can increase your church's membership and finances, or is your primary concern how you can positively invoke

---

16. Walker and Walker, "Top 5 Reasons Black Millennials Are Leaving the Church."

social change in the community within your midst? Are you more concerned with the income or outcome?

In the Black church, typically during a preacher's close, they would ask the congregation to grab their neighbor by the hand and to shake 'em, and rock 'em, rock 'em, and shake 'em. Well, today, I'd like you to use your spiritual imagination if you will, and picture those in the community who need you the most. Imagine me in front of them, a product of the hood who feels ignored by you, who found success because of those around me and recognizes the depth of work left to do, vocalizing in my best homiletical tune-up to the key of E-flat on behalf of those wandering along an unsure path:

> *It's time, preachers, for you to grab your community by the hand, letting them know that the church stands in solidarity for justice. It's time for you to stop allowing these phony politicians the opportunity to pimp and parade about in your pulpit only when they need the constituent votes of your congregation! It's time for you to grab social injustice, corruption, poverty, and systemic oppression by the horns, and shake 'em and rock 'em, rock 'em and shake 'em, until social injustice finally becomes social justice. Shake 'em and rock 'em, rock 'em and shake 'em until corruption becomes compassion! Shake 'em and rock 'em, rock 'em and shake 'em until poverty becomes equity! Shake 'em and rock 'em, rock 'em and shake 'em until systemic oppression is transformed into a social opportunity for the hood. Remember, faith is an essential need in this fight for justice and the development of under-resourced communities!*

Now before I conclude this chapter on faith, I must also address the church at large. Many church buildings closed during the 2020 pandemic. This raises a question. How much of the funds that your church saved from not having to spend on utilities and other normal expenses due to the pandemic were reallocated to community ministry programming? How much was used to help further the cause of social justice? How much was used to provide PPE for your congregation and community?

How many of you opened up your empty buildings for the homeless or to help provide life readiness skills for members of the community during this pandemic? How many of your pastors requested raises and special allowances, though their responsibilities decreased during the pandemic? How many of you gladly approved those extra funds to be allocated to your pastor while there were struggling families right down the street who truly needed such resources? Are you worshiping your pastor more than Christ? Do you have the humility and self-awareness to admit it if the answer is yes? And if so, what are you going to do about it?

One of the biggest issues within the church that has not only hindered spiritual growth but has cut off the connection between the church and the hood is, again, the church's mirroring a glorified social club rather than a spiritual hospital. Not only that, but deacons, trustees, and laypersons alike kiss up to their pastors so much, yet turn their noses up to those whom the bible would describe as the least of these within society. We've become so caught up in our fancy suits and Sunday's best attire that we've allowed our spiritual eye to be blinded.

I assume that many of you reading this specific chapter may have said ouch more than amen. You may even be offended. Even though these words may cut deep, it is my hope that they help bridge the gap between the church and the hood.

Strategies to Connect Church and Community

1. Have your pastor or official board conduct a 6-month to yearlong listening tour between the church leaders and the community.

2. Allot a minimum of 20% of your church's budget to go towards youth development programming.

3. Allot a minimum of 30% of your church's budget to go towards ministry.

4. Substitute some of your special events and anniversaries with community bonding initiatives.

5. Hold educational sessions within your church, keeping the community up to date on what's going on in the world and how they can hold their public officials accountable.

6. "Buy Back the Block" and create opportunities for community members to also obtain ownership within your community.

7. Lead from the frontlines in this fight for social justice and change!

Economics

Ask 10 people and you'll get 10 different answers: What was the United States of America built on? Some people will say life, liberty, and the pursuit of happiness. Others may point to the industrial revolution. Still, others will say freedom in general, but it's uncommon to find two people who can agree on the limits of those freedoms or whether there should even be any. And then there are those who will say hard work, but it's a rare day when you'll come across the person who'll be honest or informed about whose hard work that was.

In 2016, Michelle Obama said, "I wake up every morning in a house that was built by slaves," and she was right—the White House was indeed built by slaves, in addition to the U.S. Capitol, the Smithsonian Institution in Washington, D.C., the wall that Wall Street was named after (which was also the location for one of the country's largest slave markets), Trinity Church in New York, Ft. Sumter in South Carolina, Harvard Law School, and Georgetown University, just to name a few.[17]

Additionally, slavery was the first big business in our nation, and it laid the foundation for the U.S. to become a capitalistic powerhouse. The truth is, we have those who were enslaved to thank for our country's economic standing today, but the enslaved and their descendants haven't received anything to show for it. We were promised 40 acres and a mule but ended up with Jim Crow and chitlin's, and today's racial wealth gap is the consequence of the lack of payback.

---

17. Pasley, "15 American Landmarks That Were Built by Enslaved People."

As it stands, white Americans' average per capita wealth is $338,093, while that of Black Americans is $60,126. We make up 13.6% of the population, and we only hold 4% of the wealth. To put it in perspective, let's take a look at what constitutes wealth.

To calculate wealth, take the total market value of all your physical and intangible assets, then subtract all the debts. Considering that the average black household earns around half what the white household does:[18]

> The incidence of debt in 2019 was not markedly different among families with heads of different races/ethnicities. Just over three-quarters (77.7 percent) of families with white, non-Hispanic heads reported having debt, while 72.2 percent of families with a Hispanic head, 74 percent with a Black/African American head, and 77.6 with other heads did so. However, this is where the similarities end when it comes to debt across race/ethnicity.
>
> For example, the median debt-to-asset ratios for Black/African American and Hispanic heads were more than 50 percent higher than that of families with white, non-Hispanic heads: 46.8 percent and 46.2 percent, respectively, compared with 29.5 percent. Higher debt-to-asset ratios mean that families with minority heads had fewer resources than families with white, non-Hispanic heads to pay off debt by using assets if their income is insufficient, increasing the potential for financial fragility.
>
> One cause of the much higher debt-to-asset ratios of families with Black/African American and Hispanic heads is that, while these families had a similar likelihood of having credit card debt to that of families with white, non-Hispanic heads, they had significantly lower probabilities of having housing debt. In other words, the debt of families with minority heads was less likely to come with the

---

18. Aladangady, "Wealth Inequality and the Racial Wealth Gap."

tangible asset of a home — an asset that can help build financial wealth.

Another alarming feature of the debt of families with minority heads: These families — particularly those with Hispanic heads — were more likely to have debt payments exceeding 40 percent of their income. More than 1 in 10 (12.7 percent) of these families exceeded this threshold compared with 6.5 percent of the families with white, non-Hispanic heads.

The bottom line is that despite families with minority heads having similar likelihoods of having debt, the nature of the debt and the proportion of that debt relative to assets is more likely to result in worse financial situations than those of families with white, non-Hispanic heads.[19]

Why is it that our people are so far behind? Time. Because of slavery, racism, and genocide, whites had a 400-year head start to accumulate wealth in this country. We've all heard people talk about breaking generational curses. We've seen people go from poverty to millions in a matter of years, and sometimes, months. If you just consider the average amount of money a person or family earns in a lifetime, and what that means in terms of building wealth for their families in the future, 400 years can feel like an eternity.

Wealth and power often go hand in hand, and while it's true you can have wealth without much power, those with power always have wealth, and they also determine where it comes from and who gets more of it. The power dynamics in this country are designed as a cycle that creates barriers of entry to that wealth for those who don't have it and to gate-keep those who benefit from racism and privilege that were embedded in this country's systems from the start. For proof of this, drive around affluent neighborhoods and look at the schools. Then, do the same

---

19. EBRI. Fast Facts.

thing in the hood. Take it a step further and consider what each set of students does after school, what they go home to, who's there waiting for them, and even what they eat.

Just like wealth and power go hand in hand, so do wealth and health. Health is a branch of intersection within the roots of wealth. Drive around those neighborhoods again. Which ones have liquor stores, payday loan businesses, and dollar stores versus banks, music schools, and Whole Foods? Health and wealth are very much connected; when you have the former, it's easier to acquire the latter. The old adage, "You are what you eat," is cliché for a reason.

Think about the typical diet of a Black American and the diseases we could avoid that come with high-priced medications that usually just lead to more medications. The money we spend on those medicines, the doctors who prescribe those medicines, and the food and liquor that lead us to those doctors could be used to establish and build our wealth. Instead of building lasting inheritances, we're building illnesses that start to look hereditary, when really the only thing that's hereditary is the habits.

Money habits are also passed down from generation to generation. How many Black people do you know who are prepared to leave an inheritance to those they'll leave behind? In terms of the land and other assets we have compared to our white counterparts, we don't have it. It seems that generally, when we get it, we try to spend it as fast as we can for ourselves. Developing the discipline of delayed gratification could multiply our attempts to cover the ground we lost during slavery.

In today's landscape, anybody can know anything they want to know. Information is available for us; we just have to get it and apply it. The application of knowledge is wisdom, and wisdom can take us, as a people, from struggle to triumph. It doesn't mean anything to have the best car on the block but no 401k, stocks, or investments. What good does it do your family if you blow money every time you get paid and have nothing to leave them when you're gone? Building wealth takes discipline and the will to fight tools of oppression, but the fight is already lost when every dollar goes to rent, clothes, cars, and bills, so that by the time expenses are taken care of, there's nothing left to build with.

We need clarity of mind and a plan. When we're healthy, physically and mentally, we can more easily improve our financial health as well.

Since I believe the church historically has been a pillar of the community, I think it's important to highlight the church's role in our community's current economic standing. When preached correctly, the Bible provides sound information for wealth building, but unfortunately, too many churches aren't making such teaching a priority. Many preach poverty from the pulpit, citing, "The last shall be first and the first shall be last," convincing their congregations that rich folks can't get into heaven. They do this while they pimp out and exploit the church to fund their own one-way flights towards wealth.

When leaders care more about an income rather than the outcome of saving souls and pouring into communities, they don't mind exploiting those around them who are in dire straits and taking their money to pad their own pockets. These same funds could be building the community up, lifting us up together, but greed is selfish. A tremendous opportunity churches have to add real value to their communities is to look into establishing credit unions so we're helping our people without them having to worry about being declined for credit. At credit unions, they can get reasonable interest rates so they're not borrowing themselves into a hole they can never get out of.

We can't rely on one entity to handle this for us, however. Even if the church doesn't cooperate as a whole, we can cooperate with each other in our everyday lives. The Black dollar circulates in Black communities for an average of six hours. Think about it: if someone in the community possesses a dollar when they drop their child off at school, there's a good chance it'll be outside the community by the time the child leaves their last class of the day. That's not much time to build anything on that dollar. However, in other communities, dollars circulate for days or weeks. We need to spend our money in our own communities. White America knows this, which is why they take our ideas and resell them to us, and we buy them, rarely giving thought to what any of it means.

I'm 100% a proponent of buying Black and paying well. If you don't go into Gucci or Macy's asking for discounts, don't do it to our brothers and sisters who are trying to make a living. Likewise, if we expect good quality and service from Gucci and Macy's, we should expect our brothers and sisters to provide good quality and service to us when we buy from them. Our prices should match the quality of what we have to offer, and whatever we do, we need to always do it with excellence.

There are opportunities everywhere for us to improve our financial situations. For those of us who already have, wealth can be a blessing and a curse. It's a blessing for obvious reasons, but it can be a burden when family members expect to benefit from our success. Instead of constantly giving and feeling like a crutch, teach family and friends to acquire the wealth you've amassed. If you have the means, remove barriers for those who are coming after you. Can you pay for a nephew or cousin's education?

Can you pay for trade school? College visits? Travel opportunities? Set aside time to teach them money lessons. Take them to work with you. If you continue to give and give, you run the risk of losing wealth instead of building it. You also risk other able-bodied people getting complacent if they don't have to earn it for themselves. Complacency is another hurdle that can hinder Black wealth and growth.

One thing about young people is they're rarely complacent by nature. With youth comes hope, excitement, and aspiration. When they see something they think they can do themselves, they pour everything into it. Their wheels start turning and their creativity opens doors in their minds before they have a chance to open those doors with their hands. While sports and entertainment are exciting futures, it's unfortunate that these are the fields where most of our youth see people who look like them. I support young people's aspirations for success in sports and entertainment, but they should know those aren't the only pathways.

They should know the slim probability of making it in those fields and feel the freedom to explore the hundreds of other possibilities that can be just as rewarding and exciting. The same way they consistently see "themselves" on fields and movies, we need to find ways to show them what it looks like to be in board rooms, on Wall Street, and in the superintendent's office. Consistency is key to any achievement. White America sees our Black boys in jail-- slavery 2.0--where our children become their tools. Therefore, we must make sure they know they can use their most valuable tools, their minds, to increase their own wealth instead of allowing the systems around us to exploit their talent and drive while the rest of our community just gets the bones.

Strategies to Build Economic Wealth in Today's Landscape

1. Acquire land.

2. Educate ourselves on financial literacy starting at a young age.

3. Learn about how to leverage our credit and how to use debt to create wealth.

4. Be intentional about what credit goes in our names and use that credit to acquire appreciating resources instead of depreciating resources.

5. Learn how to make our money make more money.

6. Fight for more equitable pay and living arrangements.

7. Take care of our bodies.

8. Add children to our credit at a young age so their credit can be established by the time they graduate and/or get an LLC in their name.

Accountability

The quote, "Commitment without currency is counterfeit!" has resounded in my spirit for some time. When living in a society of watered-down promises, phony politicians, and businesses and institutions utilizing empty public relations tactics around diversity and inclusion, it's apparent that there is a dire need for accountability in our society's framework. While it may seem like there were times when we had more of it, the truth is it's always been lacking. From day one, this country has been drowning in hypocrisy.

We claim to be one nation under God, indivisible, but we are one of the most divided nations in the world. We claim to have liberty and justice for all, but ask Breonna Taylor's family if that's the American reality. Our justice system seems to have an affinity for those who lack melanin in their skin. For decades, America has waged a systemic war against the Black family, utilizing the justice system as a racist tool of oppression. Without batting an eye, we've separated children from their families (from the days of selling Blacks as slaves on the auction block to now) and held them in cages like zoo animals. Law enforcement officers swear the oath:

> I will maintain courageous *calm* in the fact of danger, scorn or ridicule; develop *self-restraint* and be constantly *mindful* of the *welfare of others*. Honest in thought and deed both in my

personal and official list, and I will be ***exemplary*** in ***obeying*** the law and the regulations of my department.[20]

While the oath sounds good on paper, its sentiment rarely makes it past the paper it's written on when it's time to confront Black people. For decades, police officers have murdered unarmed Black citizens, knowing full well they could lean on their privilege to avoid accountability.

Politicians could do something about such inequities, but it's hard to believe they want to when we've been fighting the same problems for decades. When it's campaign time, they paint pictures of change and altruism and how they plan to pour into the hood. Then, as soon as the election is over, so is the promise. They're nowhere to be seen. The care and attention our neighborhoods get are minimal, but the taxes aren't. Urban neighborhoods are overly-taxed, which steadily increases foreclosure rates.

Here, in the richest nation in the world, citizens lack clean water. Look at Flint, Michigan and Jackson, Mississippi. In both instances, drive 10 minutes in either direction of the poorest neighborhoods, and you'll find water that's safe to drink straight from the faucet. There are potholes in Detroit older than me and others in New Orleans deeper than the height of a sixth grader. Our public school systems in many urban neighborhoods are failing our children and exasperating our teachers. We all know that if these same problems existed in white neighborhoods, they wouldn't last long enough for us to even know about them. All this is possible because there is no accountability in the equation of equality.

From a radical social justice perspective, accountability is more than taking responsibility for one's actions; it's going a step further and taking action to repair any harm caused by those actions. But to repair harm, you must admit fault, and that's where pride stands in the way.

---

20. "Law Enforcement Code of Ethics." Emphasis added.

Our leaders would rather pretend like nothing was never wrong than to right a wrong. That's why they want to erase our blood-tinged history to begin with. If we ever hope to see the equity, or even its cousin, equality, that this nation claims to be based on, we have to rock the systems that uphold the problems we see today.

Racialequitytools.org defines accountability in this context as, "creating processes and systems that are designed to help individuals and groups to be held in check for their decisions and actions and for whether the work being done reflects and embodies racial justice principles."[21] To make sure actions are aligned, those in power and those working for change should be consistently asking:

- How is the issue being defined?

- Who is defining it?

- Who is this work going to benefit if it succeeds?

- Who will benefit if the work does not succeed?

- How are risks distributed among the stakeholders?

- How will a group know if its plan has accounted for risks and unintended consequences for different racial and ethnic groups?

- What happens if people pull out before the goals are met?

- Who anointed the people and groups being relied on for the answers to these questions?

- Who else can answer these questions to guide the work?[22]

To get those in power to be willing to regularly answer these questions honestly would be a massive feat, but doing so is more likely at a local level than a federal level. That's why those on the front lines of change

---

21. "Plan, Change Process, Accountability."
22. Ibid.

have to push towards these ideals consistently. They are where change happens. One would think that wouldn't be the case, given our elected officials are supposed to be accountable to those who put them in office, but too often, they get in office and forget about those who put them there. Therefore, we must learn to rely on ourselves.

Every individual within a community should be held accountable to everybody else. Sadly, public officials often get too caught up in the celebrity of their positions over the work, and we see the results of that when we drive down the street, or when the results of taxes don't match tax rates, or in a plethora of other areas where we lack even though it isn't supposed to be this way. For too long, politicians have tokenized our trauma and poverty for their own gain. When there is no accountability, we end up with under-resourced communities. Where there aren't enough resources, growth potential is hindered in the community at-large. How can people strive to be their best selves when their most basic needs aren't met? This takes us back to Maslow's Hierarchy of Needs, and those in power know that, which explains why they aren't in any hurry to make things right. Imagine an America with a self-realized populace. Now, imagine what that would mean for the power of the powers that be.

Now, this isn't to say there isn't any accountability anywhere. We don't live in anarchy. Look in the crevices in your community and you're bound to see accountability in action throughout. We see it in Block Clubs, community organization efforts, D9 (Black Greek Lettered) organizations, and grassroots organizations that are people-powered and people-focused. We see it in sound parenting in the household and good coaching in community sports leagues.

Every community has teachers and administrators who are doing their best for their students because they know the power of education. The need is not any accountability at all; the need is for an increase of accountability in our school boards and city councils, especially when they focus more on the development of downtown and uptown rather than those who are too easily forgotten in the inner-city.

When you can see the pain and lack around you and feel nothing, that signals a major lack of emotional intelligence, which is *the capacity to be aware of, control, and express one's emotions, and to handle interpersonal relationships judiciously and empathetically*. Emotional maturity is the act of applying that knowledge. It's hard to believe, when one takes the time to scan the realities of the hood, that political leaders and others who have the means have much emotional intelligence or emotional maturity. Those who will make a difference possess both. It's possible that people go into politics and other seemingly noble professions with the right ideas but too easily become contaminated by the corruption surrounding them.

We need leaders who possess the skills to make a change as well as the emotional wherewithal to see that change through, no matter what it takes.

I am a firm believer of the Talented Tenth, and I believe mentorship has the power to break any barrier and push us towards a society truly filled with equity. The "Talented Tenth" is a concept championed by W.E.B. DuBois that refers to the "one in ten Black men [who] have cultivated the ability to become leaders of the Black community by acquiring a college education, writing books, and becoming directly involved in social change."[23] The responsibility of this remnant was to "sacrifice their personal interests and endeavors to provide leadership for the African American community."[24]

This concept is an attractive one because it speaks to unity, teamwork, and selflessness, qualities that scream of a person's possession of emotional intelligence and maturity. I believe no one is "self-made." There's no way we can ever make it without the participation of others

---

23. Wikipedia contributors, "Talented Tenth."
24. Battle and Wright, "W.E.B. Du Bois's Talented Tenth."

on some level. It takes mentorship and leadership, someone pouring into you, to achieve the heights of your capabilities and fully walk in your purpose. When we adopt the adage, "Each one teach one, each one reach one," we begin to operate in multiplication. We build leaders who build leaders and people who hold purpose instead of grudges. When we can look around and see this as the norm, we will begin to establish lasting change.

We need to make accountability a value in every home. We need to demonstrate it in our workplaces. If we as a community don't push for it in schools, our children's education will be lacking, and they will suffer the effects forever. We must hold ourselves, our children, our teachers, and our school administrators accountable in this facet of our lives. When we do that, when we demand an education that lives up to our dreams and our potential, when we teach our children what they need to know concerning their language, math, history, finances, science, and the arts, we will finally have the power to stop the pipeline that reaches from Black American neighborhoods straight to the local detention centers and ends at the prisons.

According to The Sentencing Project, "Black Americans are incarcerated in state prisons at nearly five times the rate of white Americans," and "one in 81 Black adults in the U.S. is serving time in state prison."[25] Most prisoners are between the ages of 26 and 50 years old,[26] prime earning years. Do Black Americans go to prison at five times the rate of white Americans because they commit five times the crime? Absolutely not. Of all the arrests in 2019 in America, 69.4% were white offenders and 26.6% were Black.[27]

This number still may be a poor indicator when you consider who was arrested and shouldn't have been and who wasn't when they should have

25. Nellis, "The Color of Justice: Racial and Ethnic Disparity in State Prisons."
26. "BOP Statistics: Average Inmate Age."
27. "Table 43."

been, but these are the best numbers we have to go by. Our country is one that has a long history of incarcerating Black men, starting with slavery and carrying on into slave patrols, Jim Crow laws, Stop and Frisk laws, and everyday profiling. If we make thorough education a priority and focus on the hope that comes with that, and when we expose our young people to the professional possibilities around them–from tech to education, from finance to real estate, from culinary arts to music, and the plethora of options in between–they start to see that there's more to life than what they're used to seeing, and we can then put a kink in the pipeline that leads to nowhere but hopelessness.

If we refuse to hold ourselves and each other accountable, we are sacrificing our future. We will succumb to our foolishness and pride, and power, privilege, and oppression will win. We must lead with humility and accountability, and more specifically, cultural humility, which has three primary principles:

1. Lifelong learning and critical self-reflection
2. Recognition of and challenge to power imbalances
3. Modeling of institutional accountability.

When we look around and see how others model their cultural experiences, we can recognize our own culture's blind spots, and in doing so, we can facilitate a demonstration of respect and a sense of equality. This can't just be on an individual level; institutions must also be self-reflective. Cultural humility serves to recognize power imbalances that are inherent in institutions and assumes the accountability to mitigate them. Understanding institutions should begin with children when they are young, and Block Clubs, like youth councils, in our neighborhoods are the perfect starting point.

This way, the hood can collectively hold its city accountable while creating a training ground for our youth to familiarize themselves with the way the system operates on an official level, such as with Roberts

Rules of Order, lobbying, and other tools to mold them to carry the torch of change around them at the micro and macro levels.

When politicians come to your church, job, or neighborhood, make the youth pay attention. Have them record the promises these people so easily make and show them how to hold them to their work if they're elected. Never be afraid to ask questions, especially the questions that make people uncomfortable. Comfort zones never produce change. It's time to get out of our comfort zones and into the realm of accountability and action! We have to get to a point where our word is our bond. If our words have lost their value, it's time to get that value back.

Strategies to Establish Accountability as a Core Value

1. Form neighborhood groups to implement and maintain the change we want to see on a micro level.

2. Groom a worthy candidate from the hood to run for office.

3. Stay involved in politics after the election is over.

4. Make accountability a core value in your homes and places of work.

5. Use Block Clubs to teach the youth how to run meetings and organize initiatives in their communities.

Ubuntu

I was in college when I learned about Ubuntu, and it's been a staple value of mine ever since.

A Zulu word that means "humanness," Zulu's main principle is, "a person is a person through other persons." It means we cannot do it alone. It also means whatever we do to other people will come back to us. Every aspect of community is encapsulated in this concept. Its central ethics are:

- Reciprocity--exchange for mutual benefit. This is the only way relationships work and people can feel they're not being taken for granted. When everyone is doing their part, everyone benefits, everyone feels useful, and no one feels used. People feel like they and their efforts have value when others show appreciation and give what they have to offer to the cause as well. Additionally, when we operate in reciprocity, we get to see the parts of the whole come together in beautiful ways. When we see this happen, we can't help but to feel that we're doing what we were put on this planet to do, because knowing where we fit in the world and seeing it in action brings about a sense of belonging.

- Common good--What's best for everybody or the majority? That's the common good. The Catechism notes three essential elements of the common good:

- Respect for the individual
- The social well-being and development of the group
- Peace that stems from the stability of a just society

It seems that these three elements cover everything, and it doesn't seem like anything that's too difficult to do, but when ego and self get in the way, people become incapable of respect for those who aren't like them or who they don't view as human; they become unconcerned about the social well-being and development of the group; and peace, stability, and justice become mere buzzwords they use to get more of what they want: power.

- Peaceful relations--Look around; there's war and pain everywhere. Where there isn't war, there is the threat of war. If the war isn't country to country, it's political party to political party, or race to race, or within the family structure. Sometimes it seems that there are very few people who value peace at all, and while this may not be true, it sure is hard to find (sometimes even in your own home). There are many benefits to keeping peace at bay. War is big business; it makes a lot of people a lot of money. Discord makes for excellent entertainment, whether it be in music, movies, on stages, or in the streets for passersby to watch and film. There are entire careers built purely on conflict. Peace starves capitalism, therefore, those who love money find a way to keep it away. James Baldwin wrote, "I would like us to do something unprecedented, to create ourselves without finding it necessary to create an enemy." This is the sign of an evolved society, one that we can create. While we may not see this fully realized on a national level, we can create environments of peace in our communities.

- Human dignity--Dignity is a sense of pride, honor, and respect. Those who have it exude it, and when a person values themselves, it's much easier to value someone else. Pride, honor, and respect put us in a mental position to want to succeed, to believe in ourselves and others, and to establish and spread the spirit of Ubuntu.

- Value of human life--When we believe we should treat people a certain way simply because they are human, we treat people like they matter. We put their health and well-being above all else. We show empathy when we see people hurting and go out of our way to help when we see they're in pain or struggling in some way. When we don't value human life, we're unconcerned about what others are going through. There's an attitude of, "I gotta get mine, you gotta get yours," instead of the desire to link arms and move through the world together. When we value human life, the last thing we want to do is to hurt someone else, physically, emotionally, or in any other way. We use our experiences to elevate others. This is the essence of Ubuntu.

- Consensus--Consensus, or agreement, is an extension of peaceful relations. Can we get in a room and make decisions for the greater good without allowing pride to distract us?

- Do we possess the knowledge of our people on an individual level as well as a community level to understand what's best and to act on it, even if everyone doesn't get everything they want? When we can agree, we make progress. When we can't agree, we fall apart.

- Tolerance--Tolerance is, "the capacity to endure pain or hardship; endurance, fortitude, stamina; sympathy or indulgence for beliefs or practices differing from or conflicting with one's own; the act of allowing something; toleration."[28] Everybody around us will not be like us. It cannot happen. We are all individuals with individual thoughts. Although the masses might move in one direction, we are allowed to think differently, and if

---

28. "Definition of Tolerance."

someone thinks differently, we need to learn how to listen to their viewpoints and be willing to accept them as part of the whole, even if we disagree. There are some instances that would make this exceedingly difficult. It's a waste of time to try to make someone agree with you, and it's a waste of time to try to work with someone who's determined to stand against you, but if someone has the same bottom-line goal and similar ideas of how to get there, it's important to tolerate the differences for the greater good. This leads us to the last value.

- Mutual respect--Respect, which is admiration or regard for someone else, has to be extended from one person to another. Respect is the root through which every other value of Ubuntu grows and thrives.

The people of Sub-Saharan Africa live by these ideals to inform their beliefs, attitudes, and practices. As a result, they place heavy emphasis on harmony in the community, hospitality, social cohesion/interdependence, friendliness, and compassion. Ubuntu means, "I am because we are."

This concept is vastly different from the "look out for number one" attitude and overwhelming personal pride and focus on nationalism in front of our faces in America each day. When our people first arrived on this soil, we had a much greater spirit of Ubuntu among us, and while I wouldn't say we've lost that spirit, I do believe it's been dampened throughout the generations. In fact, I'd go as far as to say the reason it is not strong within us and spreading from generation to generation is because we simply don't talk about it enough to give it the energy it needs to thrive. In the past few years especially, we've heard the concept of "letting go of anything that doesn't serve us," and many people go as far as to sever relationships with well-meaning, albeit annoying, family members or friends, a sentiment that is a far cry from that of tolerance and peaceful relations and acceptance.

But of course, all is not lost. Our community can be one that reflects the essence of who our people have always been historically; we just need to talk about and live "we are" much more than the common concept of "I am."

The power of Ubuntu could transform those of us living on American soil, and it can spread its influence much further. We need this to happen. Sadly, the Black diaspora is divided. We have pitted ourselves against each other in what sometimes feels like a competition of "true Blackness." The strife that exists between Africans and Black Americans does nothing to serve us. In fact, it furthers the efforts of those who want nothing more than to see us fail by pushing unity further away. Those who aren't Black Americans try to separate themselves from us, which hurts all of us more than it helps any of us.

Those who aren't Americans make the argument that we who make our home in the United States are not really Black folk. They claim we don't know our history, that we believe the lies white America has told us about them (like they swing from trees and are otherwise uncivilized), and that we lack any true culture. Some even argue that we didn't come back "home" after the Transatlantic Slave Trade, as if we would have even known where "home" was for us, or like our people did not and could not have established a new life on the soil where they were. Oftentimes, they align with the "model minority" ideas that white people try to use to elevate successful non-whites, putting them on a pedestal and trying to use them as an example of what other minorities, namely Black folks, could become if only we'd truly apply ourselves.

Our African brothers and sisters are sometimes tempted by this rhetoric and also question why Black Americans aren't as successful as they are, not realizing that they've gotten here by vastly different circumstances than we did, and they haven't had to pay the Black tax like we have as a result of growing up in the American system. They get to bypass the systemic hurdles in ways that we don't. The riff is clear. We don't give each other the time of day because we see and hear each other, make decisions about who the other person is, and miss opportunities to weave a small thread of unity while choosing to replace it with enmity that keeps us all in last place.

Many figures throughout our history demonstrated what Ubuntu looks like. Dr. Huey P. Newton, Fred Hampton, and Stokley Carmichael of the Black Panther Party were excellent examples of the concept. The Party had a ten-point program through which they operated, the ten points, abbreviated, being:

1. We want freedom.

2. We want full employment for our people.

3. We want an end to the robbery by the capitalists of our Black community.

4. We want decent housing fit for the shelter of human beings.

5. We want education for our people that exposes the true nature of this decadent American society.

6. We want all Black men to be exempt from military service.

7. We want an immediate end to police brutality and the murder of Black people.

8. We want freedom for all Black men held in federal, state, county, and city prisons and jails.

9. We want all Black people when brought to trial to be tried in a court by a jury of their peer group or people from their Black communities, as defined by the Constitution of the United States.

10. We want land, bread, housing, education, clothing, justice, and peace.[29]

---

29. BlackPast, "(1966) The Black Panther Party Ten-Point Program •"

The Panthers lived this out through their actions every day in the following ways:

- Their free breakfast programs provided a full free breakfast for more than 20,000 students in 19 cities before they went to school each day.

- They established free medical centers in 13 cities to test for high blood pressure and other illnesses and provide treatment for those illnesses and physicals for general health.

- The Panthers started Seniors Against a Fearful Environment to protect senior citizens in the community after the Oakland Police Department refused to look after them.

- They provided free, rapid transportation to the hospital without checking into the patient's financial status through the People's Free Ambulance Service.

- They established the Free Food Program which supplemented groceries to those who couldn't afford it.

- They established The Black Student Alliance to create programs at educational institutions to unify the student body, namely Black students.

- The Black Panther newspaper shared information about chapters throughout the country, news of oppressed communities around the world, theoretical writing, and any news about the liberation of humanity.

The Panthers were powerful and steadily gaining momentum, so the government killed its leaders. We cannot operate in the fear of the same fate. The survival of our community depends on this kind of courage and grit to prevail. Other figures who embodied Ubuntu are Dr. King, Shirley Chisolm, A. Philip Randolph, Bayard Rustin, Dorothy Height, Robert Sengstacke, Gwendolyn Brooks, Jane Bolin, and Cornel West.

We, as a people, must be aware of all the divisions between us and make the conscious decision to disallow those divisions to hold any further power over us. We are divided by skin tone, we are divided by nationality, and sadly, we are often divided by gender.

The division between men and women in our community has been a problem since slavery and has not yet been rectified. Instead of fighting about who has it better or worse, it is our responsibility to stop arguing in circles about what each side has to offer, take up the concepts of Ubuntu, and unify so that our race's foundation can become unshakeable.

If your knowledge of Black America fails to extend beyond what we learn in a typical classroom, your knowledge of your history will be severely lacking. We come from the bloodlines of leaders, kings, queens, inventors, trailblazers, brilliance. Alone, we are merely a drop in a bucket, but together, we're an ocean that can move mountains and shift valleys. We need to push the philosophy of Ubuntu throughout Black America and the diaspora as a whole. Any division rips away our oneness, which is our strength. Through Ubuntu, we can overcome anything and everything that oppresses us. The shackles that are set up to fracture and bind us can be overcome.

<u>Strategies for fostering a spirit of ubuntu in the community:</u>

1. Get in the mindset of reciprocity and the common good in all we do.

2. Make our homes a place of peace. What happens in the home permeates everywhere else.

3. Practice non-violent communication and listening skills.

4. Be open to viewpoints different from your own.

5. Understand the misunderstandings between Black Americans and Africans so you know how to combat misconceptions

6. Refuse to back down when faced with pushback from powerful entities

7. Educate and organize.

Representation

Representation. It's a sign that those in powerful positions see you as one who belongs to society. It's a marker that somebody who looks and lives like you has a place in the spaces you want to be. It's an opportunity to tell your story your way.

For years, when you looked at movies, television shows, commercials, and advertisements, it was a rare thing to see anybody of color, and if you saw them, they were either in the background, or they were in the foreground doing something negative or taboo. Many people in the entertainment industry have fought long and hard to do something about this, and while we've come a long way, we still have a long way to go. However, the boom of ethnic and racial representation that has taken place since the turn of the century has certainly been notable. Time will tell of its long-term effects, but we can immediately celebrate the positive results of the presence of Black people in the vast landscape of media today.

The value of ethnic and racial representation is priceless because the media presents a narrative. That narrative creates a perception, and perception is reality in the eyes of those who are watching. If you never witness Black people doing much in everyday life, but you see them doing things on television all the time, what you see on television is what will weave your belief about that people group. Even if it's not blatant, the subconscious picks up on details and correlations, and if there is little to no positive representation, deeply-held beliefs can be woven out of the distant portrayals brought to you by television.

Through the use of such psychological tactics, the media has often been a tool of both power and oppression, and it's been utilized to create narratives that sometimes uplift the Black community and other times tear it down. The value of the media can never be overstated.

Positive media representation can help increase the self-esteem of those in marginalized groups, especially the youth of those groups. Additionally, interpersonal contact and exposure through media presence can help reduce stereotypes in those groups, which can, in turn, contribute to the safety and humanization of those who are often portrayed negatively. However, when done without thought and input from representatives of these demographics, representation can be filled with racial microaggressions, implicit biases, and skewed viewpoints.

When the media reports something positive in Detroit, they refer to the area as "Metro Detroit" to include the areas where white counterparts live and move. However, when something negative occurs, like a murder or some other crime, the media subtracts the word "metro" and simply says, "Detroit," and then they proceed to give the exact location of where the catastrophe occurred. Pay attention to how the media relays information about murderers, thieves, and robbers when they're from a city with a high population of Black citizens or when the perpetrator is Black or otherwise marginalized.

The details about that person, especially any wrong move in their life's history—no matter how major or minor—are put on full display. But if that person is white, the details shared about their lives do more to protect the perpetrator than to convict or damn them. Messages like this sway public perception. The good thing about the technological world we live in now is we have the ability to film, show, and see the unadulterated truth.

Had it not been for cameras, Derek Chauvin could have easily gotten away with the slaughter of George Floyd, the murder that added new fire to the Black Lives Matter movement in 2020, especially since he'd been the subject of over 22 complaints and investigations during his 19 years as a cop in Minneapolis.[30] Nineteen years before George Floyd, everyone didn't have cameras and access to the entire world via social media at the palm of their hands. Now, we do, and because of this, many other criminals' acts unfold right in front of our eyes, creating an important type of accountability for the decision-makers in this country.

What is often lacking when it comes to representation is intentionality. Without intention, it's easy for tokenism to creep in. Tokenism is a powerful tool because it relieves the need for nuance. Without nuance, it's very easy to slide a person into a category that makes the world easier to understand, despite how off-base that understanding may be. If someone tells you and shows you incessantly that Black people are bad and dangerous, in order to protect yourself, it's easiest to accept the message and make sure you're on high alert when you're around Black people, even if a Black person has never done anything against you, and even if someone of your same race has.

When you see people who look like you as examples of goodness, your mind makes the correlation that people who look like you are good. However, with honest, intentional representation, everyone watching sees that people are people, and race is no determinant of goodness. People love to throw around the words of Dr. Martin Luther King Jr. as if he wanted a nation of people who are "color blind," but when he said he hoped one day people would be judged by the content of their character instead of the color of their skin, what he meant was that people wouldn't be elevated or condemned because of the color of their skin; what he meant was that we should be judged as individuals, because everybody who looks like you isn't good, and everybody who doesn't look like you isn't bad.

---

30. Lartey and VanSickle, "'Don't Kill Me': Others Tell of Abuse by Officer Who Knelt on George Floyd."

When representation grows from tokenism, corporations and politicians can easily tokenize our oppression and use it for personal gain while hoping we're satisfied to just see our faces on billboards or TV shows. We must refuse to allow them to pull such strings. The community's job is to expand our light and grow the connections with folks who look like us. Accountability in this space is way overdue.

Commitment without currency is counterfeit. Leaders of churches have no qualms about allowing politicians to enter their church with pomp and circumstance, saunter into their pulpits, and lie to the faces of the congregations to get votes. Then, after the election, you don't see them again until the next election cycle. Corporations are no different. If they have no equitable motivation to invest in the community and its cause, their "commitments" to equity are nothing more than marketing ploys. These things happen and continue to happen because we allow them.

When we fight back with our votes and dollars, they listen. We are the leaders whether we know it or not. America is a country of capitalism, and capitalism is about the almighty dollar. We have to voice our demands with our money and actions. Words are not enough.

Now, since we know capitalism works this way, it's easy to become cynical when we see an uptick of those in marginalized groups around us in ways and numbers we've never seen before. Some see it as nothing more than marketing, and it makes sense to be suspicious in a country that has never truly recognized your people as fully human (or human at all, depending on who and in what time period you ask). When we're only portrayed negatively, it's up to us to fight against the normative representation.

We need more movie and TV show roles of Black excellence, both individually and collectively, both stateside and abroad, and we need to ensure those roles don't disrespect us or place us in a bucket of white media propaganda. Hollywood greats have spoken out about how difficult it is to get such roles on the big screen because the perception is that people don't want to see too much of that, but the truth is if we keep demanding such roles with our dollars, that would be proof enough to producers that we want more of it.

However, part of the problem is the power lies with those with the money, and those people often don't look like us. In fact, many of the Black outlets are not even owned by Black people. Def Jam, Essence, and TVOne are examples of such outlets. Is it possible for outlets that aren't Black owned to tell our story the right way? Yes. Is it probable that they will? No. It's time that we own our media presence. Byron Allen has done tremendous work in exactly this space. The comedian-turned-media mogul owns ABC, NBC, CBS, and FOX affiliate stations, just to name a few.

When representation is executed with good motives, we can change the trajectory of our country's landscape. Done right, it puts focus on the issues we must keep top of mind to grow as a society. It connects and uplifts, forcing us to pay attention to what's going on in our own neighborhoods as well as the neighborhoods around us. We become more "we" and less "us vs. them." We are seeing Black folks en masse in the media today, not because we just became notable enough to be on television, but because those in power, or those who are taking the power into their own hands, are making it a point to tell our stories.

It's our responsibility to take control of our stories—past, present, and future. Those who have left the hood need to come back and invest, buy a home, and even live in the communities from which they came. They can be doctors, lawyers, entrepreneurs, and artists in the neighborhoods that raised them. This type of presence will create a domino effect that will push kids into their purposes because they will be able to see their future in front of them on a daily basis.

Will representation alone bring us to racial justice? Obviously not. In order for racism to truly end, representation must be accompanied by policies and practices that undo racism. Many institutions invite us in to fill a quota with no intention of ever investigating the true cause of the harm against us. No amount of representation or diversity initiatives will fix an institution if the systemic issues are not addressed, but the best thing about the media is it has the power to plant the seed, water that seed, and tell the story once the seed is in full bloom.

<u>Strategies to increase positive representation among our people:</u>

1. Be intentional. Representation without intention leads to tokenism.

2. Lead with votes. Lead with dollars. Research who you vote for and where you spend your money, and make decisions that will affect you positively.

3. Support more media that represents Black people positively, and support less that doesn't. Doing so will create the demand for more positive roles.

4. Once you've made it, stay in the neighborhood that made you. Younger generations need daily physical reminders that they can be successful.

Politics

Ask the average American if capitalism and democracy work for American society at large, and many will respond with a hearty, "Yes!" I can't help but to ask any individual who holds that belief, "For who? Who exactly does it work for?"

If one can peel away the early indoctrination of emotional lyrics of purple mountains' majesties and the unyielding bravery of those who fought and died for the freedom of the people who walk among this great American soil, and take an honest look at how this society operates, how the power dynamics were, from day one, designed to benefit white men, they would be forced to think twice about their answer to that question. Ask a Black person that question, and they would be forced to examine the operative systems of this country through the lens of "Afronomics," or economics within and relative to the Black community.

We have been taught, both overtly and covertly, that democracy reigns supreme and everybody wants it, but socialism or anything like it is unsuccessful at best and evil at worst. I believe for us to truly gain the most of what our society can offer, we have to peel back the problematic aspects of the system in which we currently operate, one that was birthed from hatred, racism, and genocide. It simply cannot prevail. However, what could prevail is a hybrid, a blend of capitalism and socialism directly connected to a new dynamic instead of the power dynamics of the European system that is our current foundation, a framework founded and resourced in justice and equality.

Is a democracy in a racist society a true democracy? How could it be? The Declaration of Independence was penned in a home that was owned by a slave driver and operated by enslaved Africans, and this irony is the lifeblood of every aspect of the American system. The USA's founding principles were supposed to embrace the ideals of freedom and equality, but still today, we are fighting the endless battles brought on by systemic exclusion, racism, and suppression of Blacks and other communities of color.

Laws in this country have done everything from preventing us from learning to read, to preventing us from owning land, to preventing us from owning patents for our inventions, to preventing us from acquiring housing. Decisions have kept us behind bars even after DNA has exonerated us, and a law is necessary for us to be able to wear our hair to work the way it grows out of our heads. How can we say with a straight face that we are a democratic nation when we have countless barriers of entry into a peaceful American life preventing certain folks from participating in normal, everyday processes?

All of this is designed to make us powerless, or at least to make us feel that way. That individual lack of power translates to a collective lack of power which translates into a lack of political power. When we lack political power, we cannot enact systems of public policy. Think of the school to prison pipeline as an example, or how the criminal justice system utilizes felonies as a tool to keep citizens from voting. In fact, consider the voting system itself and how the focus on the presidential election is all-consuming, while most people can't even tell you what positions are on the ballot for their upcoming local elections or which of their fellow citizens are running for those positions. Believe it or not, local elections affect us much more directly and much more quickly than anything that comes from the White House.

All too often, those who hold the power simply use it to continue to lynch Black Americans under the guise of law and order. The prosecutor of Michigan's Wayne County, Kym Worthy, has single-handedly targeted and jailed thousands of Black men, even though many of her cases have been shown to contain errors or misproceedings. It is vital to know who our prosecutors, attorneys, judges, mayors, and city managers are, because what they do affects us as a people in our own front yards. In fact, many states deny justice for those whose only yard is the prison yard or who have no yard at all.

Anyone who's committed a felony loses the right to vote, even after they've served their time. In many states, the homeless are turned away from the polls because of a lack of identification or address. While there are those who are working to rectify these atrocities, we still, as a society, do not discuss these issues enough. The core of a democracy is the ability to choose your leadership, but if you've broken the law or have fallen on difficult times, you no longer get to participate in your democracy. So what does that make you? Are you still a citizen?

The law suggests you're not. These Americans lose access to the rights they're promised as citizens. But then again, democracy has historically been a system of exclusion, not inclusion. This is just one of the many ways politicians work to divide and rank us. There are many other tactics at work, chief among them being the blatant division based on party lines.

The Democrat/Republican fight is one that likely won't end anytime soon, and while it's arguable whether either side has the full interest of marginalized groups at heart, there is clearly more of a focus on us from one side than the other. We look at political issues as existing on one side of the fence or the other, but all these arguments should be viewed as American issues. Since they aren't, what they end up doing is slowing down our progression. However, there are those who argue that since Blacks were the first Republicans, Blacks should be Republicans still today.

There have been several political shifts throughout history, and the en masse move of Black people from Republican to Democrat was one of them. Black people who could vote voted Republican from around the 1860s to the mid-1930s because Republicans protected voting rights. Black people saw this and other protections as a means to accomplish their goals. In fact, Frederick Douglass once said, "The Republican Party is the ship and all else is the sea around us." For most of the 19th century, the Democratic Party was about white supremacy and didn't welcome Blacks at all.

A conservative group of politicians, the Democratic Bourbons (who were also called conservatives), controlled the Southern Democratic Party well into the 20th century. They called their opponents radicals, whether they warranted the label or not.

After a while, the Republicans began to take the Black vote for granted. Additionally, not all of them supported Blacks people's right to vote. Things shifted slowly as a result of the Great Depression and policies of The New Deal, then took a sharp turn around 1965 with the passage of the Civil Rights Act. Since then, most Black voters have been loyal to the Democratic ticket.

Today's Democratic Party is one that's put prestigious Blacks in high places: Barack Obama, Stacey Adams, Kamala Harris, and countless others. Ever since we could be, Black people have been involved in politics, but we need to be so at a much larger scale. As with many powerful leaders who make the country move, Black women have led the charge in movements and change. However, since Kamala Harris left the senate to become Vice President, there are, in 2023, no Black female U.S. Senators. In the wake of BLM, we need the representation of Black women in our senate. In fact, an interview from LWV states:

> "It is now that Black women, in the spirit of Shirley Chisholm, are stepping off the sideline in realizing that we can be more than organizers and staffers and volunteers. We can also be campaign operatives, and that we too can be candidates," said Carr. "We have Black women running for governor across this

country in the deep South, to the Midwest. And we are not only looking to send one Black woman to the US Senate, but a cohort. And that is about institutional and generational change that we're normalizing Black women's leadership."[31]

This normalization is yet to be realized nationally, but as far as local leadership goes:

- A record number of Black women ran for and won congressional offices in 2020.

- Between 2020 and 2021, Black women's state legislative representation increased, though not as much as it did after the 2018 election.

- Black women reached a record high in state legislative representation in 2021.

- Black women now hold the top executive post in 8 of the 100 most populous cities, matching their proportion of the U.S. population, which is 7.8%.[32]

LWV also states that voter registration is up, however, registration often does not translate to votes on election day. We can't go halfway; we must finish the job and get out and vote. However, many people are jaded by the system, feeling as if their votes don't count. And honestly, in many ways, they don't. Consider the origins and perpetuation of the Electoral College as described by PBS:

- When the framers met for the Constitutional Convention in Philadelphia in 1787, they aimed to unify the colonies with a government that gave fair representation to all states, no matter their size.

31. https://www.lwv.org/newsroom/news-clips/power-us-black-women-deciding-elections

32. Schnall, "New Report On The State Of Black Women In American Politics Highlights Both Progress And Untapped Potential."

- They were deciding whether slaves in Southern states should be considered property –to abscond population taxes — or people, so those states could have more representation in government.

- Slaves were the economic heart and pulse of the country, and the Northern states, even if they did not engage in slavery, benefited from their labor. So even though slaves were unable to vote, the Convention decided that slaves should be counted as three-fifths of a white person for the purposes of representation in Congress.

- Considering options for electing the president, James Madison, now known as the "Father of the Constitution" and a slave-owner in Virginia, said the "right of suffrage was much more diffusive in the Northern than the Southern States; and the latter could have no influence in the election on the score of Negroes."

- With that, Madison had proposed the prototype for the same Electoral College system the country uses today: instead of a direct vote, each state was to choose electors, roughly based on their population, but weighted by slaves.

- The Convention decided the electors would convene, exchange ideas and cast their votes to reflect their own ideals on the state's behalf. Though the framers could not foresee that by 1800, Thomas Jefferson, whose state of Virginia was the largest because of its 40 percent slave population, would beat out John Adams, who was opposed to slavery.

- Jefferson also convinced his state to give him all its electoral votes if he won the majority of its ballots. Then, Jefferson signed Ohio as a state, which also gave all its electors to the most popular candidate instead of dividing them among the parties, and the Federalist party engaged in the same tactic.

- By 1823, Madison had profound distaste for this winner-take-all approach. "At the present period, the evil is at its maximum," he wrote, and called for an amendment to abandon it, but that never happened.

- It took nearly 100 years after the Convention to abolish slavery with the 13th Amendment in 1865. Later came women's suffrage in 1920, and then the prohibition of discriminatory voter registration requirements with the Civil Rights Act of 1964. By then, more than 80 percent of black voters across the country had started to favor the Democratic candidate in presidential elections.[33]

Furthermore, considering the results of the 2010 U.S. Census:

> [M]ore than half of the country's black population, about 23 million and growing, lives in the South, which is encompassed by Washington, D.C., and 15 states that stretch from Texas to Delaware, according to the 2010 U.S. Census. The Republican party won 12 of those states, and their combined 162 electoral votes, through states' winner-take-all approach to the Electoral College system in 2016.

> The Democratic party won three states — Delaware, Maryland and Virginia — as well as D.C. for a combined total of 29 electoral votes.

> "[We have] an electoral college that says to this entire voting block of people, 'You all are voting in high numbers, high turnout across the board, across the country. But in the end, that does not matter because we'll have this elector, maybe they'll do what you've done, maybe they won't,'" Sykes said.[34]

---

33. "The Racial History of the Electoral College — and Why Efforts to Change It Have Stalled."
34. Ibid.

In a system like this, that has only used us for their gain and benefit, and that failed to issue reparations that were promised to us, why should we have to pay taxes? This in itself seems like a tool of oppression, a way to force a penance to our abuser.

At times, it seems like there's more work to be done than we could ever do to point this country towards equality. In theory, that's why we elect people to powerful positions: to do the work for us. But on the whole, faith in those positions continues to dwindle at a rate much more quickly than it grows or remains steadfast.

Politics has become as commercialized as the winter holiday season. We treat politicians like celebrities, so that's what they act like. Instead of figures of valor, service, and accountability, they often behave like reality TV stars who operate off a script that fails to reflect their true efforts or intentions. Once they're sworn in, they position themselves far above the lackeys who elected them. "Service" becomes a keyword in their marketing scheme. Nothing more.

I am the Chief Hood Officer of consulting firm, Hood, Black, and Educated Consulting Group, and one of my most memorable consulting experiences—for all the wrong reasons—was working for a politician as they prepared to campaign for a congressional seat in Michigan. The candidate was notoriously late, rude, impatient, and self-centered. Why they chose to enter into politics was a mystery to me, because it was clear this person wasn't focused on what was best for the people. That people vote purely on name recognition is one of the main reasons we are in our current situation, and this was a prime example of that.

At one point, the client was two payments behind and showed up hours late for an event. When I mentioned that I needed to be paid, the response was, "You'd be lucky to get lunch out of me, let alone x amount of dollars." Despite the fact we'd entered a contract, they wrote me a check for $50 that said "Lunch" on the memo line. I was infuriated, embarrassed, and about to burst with emotion. I knew, based on how they ran their campaign, that they wouldn't make it past the primary. I was right, and that lessened the blow a bit. It also gave me a prime example of what politics and politicians should not be. Politicians need to remember, "Power to the people, for the power is the people," but it's our job to remind them of this truth.

The solution that many citizens have reached to help put caring people in political seats has been to run for office themselves in an attempt to weed out career or legacy politicians. Whether or not this is a good idea is a matter of motive. We have more than enough phony leaders in the world. We need more radical grassroots change-agents who truly are seeking change and want to make a difference in our communities, not candidates who run just to keep power in the family or to win a popularity contest for the sake of the perks and notoriety that accompany the seat.

Strategies to Influence Politics

1. Get involved. Politics affects every single aspect of your life. If you don't participate, you have no say in what happens to you.

2. Learn how today's systems came to be and why they are still surviving.

3. Find out who's running for office in the next local elections. Find out who currently holds those positions. Make it your business to know who's making the decisions in your neighborhood.

4. Consider running for office.

5. Don't just register to vote. Get out and vote on election days, and take someone with you.

Building Up the Hood

Look around hoods in many American cities, and you'll start to see new businesses like coffee shops and grocery stores, hip new apartment complexes, a facelift of surrounding buildings and roads, and fewer and fewer Black faces. This is what happens when the money comes in from the outside to build up the community. Inevitably, housing prices go up, pushing the Black folks out. This pattern is what we call "gentrification," and it's a tool of oppression and exclusion that has historically negatively affected our people through redlining and displacement.

Some may argue that gentrification is positive since it brings about opportunity and capital to low-income communities, but if that is the case, who is this opportunity designed to benefit? Ownership of the surrounding real estate plays a major role in determining whether gentrification is positive or negative for a community's existing citizens. The newest tool in this arsenal is major corporations' bullying of homeowners to push them out of their communities and the promise of development and resources that they never make good on.

For example, look at how the Little Caesars Arena in Detroit promised growth for the surrounding neighborhood but only ended up benefitting itself. The people who were already there were pushed out, and there wasn't much they could do about it. That's because gentrification is really about power.

The key to the net worth of most Americans isn't a stock portfolio, but rather the equity accumulated in their homes. It's this equity that has created generational wealth for many white Americans. This wealth can fund college educations, finance small businesses, make investments in lucrative projects, and much more. But homeownership, which is central to the American Dream, has been and remains an unequal and financially frustrating experience for many Black families. This is partially because of the difficulties that so often accompany acquiring homeownership, and partially because of what has happened all too often to those who found a way to thrive.

By 1898, Wilmington, North Carolina was a thriving city with a majority Black population. The day after the 1898 election, white people announced the "white declaration of independence," overthrew the Wilmington government, destroyed the printing press, and forced out the mayor. All of that, and it still wasn't enough to quench these men's thirst for evil. A mob of white men began to attack the city's Black residents, and as a result of this act of domestic terrorism, somewhere between 60-300 Black people were killed.

Blackbottom, Detroit was a predominantly Black neighborhood that was demolished for redevelopment in the late 1950s to early 1960s and replaced with a freeway. In 1923, a mob of 200 white men attacked Rosewood, Florida, killing over 30 Blacks, burning the community to the ground, and forcing survivors to flee. There are too many untold stories like this one, but one that has garnered tremendous attention in recent years is the Tulsa Race Massacre, or the destruction of Black Wall Street.

The year 2023 marks 102 years since the massacre in which white mobs unleashed animalistic violence against Tulsa, Oklahoma's Black citizens, institutions, and wealth. An estimated 300 people were killed, and approximately 35 acres of commercial and residential property within the Greenwood District, or what was known as Black Wall Street, were all destroyed. Before the massacre, Greenwood was a thriving hub of the Black middle class. Its citizens boasted a robust economy, and the dollar would stay within the community's households for around 19 months before it was spent elsewhere. Compare that power to today, when the Black dollar only stays in our community for a few hours. Such atrocities have lasting impacts, both physical, mental, and emotional. They stunted economic growth, and recovery from such tragedies is no easy feat.

That's why even today—especially today—it is our responsibility to be cognizant of how and where we spend our money. It must be a priority to equip our businesses with insurance and other necessary resources to protect what we're building. We must never assume that the racism of yesterday is not the racism of today. Just because these instances are not as common as they once were, just because racially motivated genocide is not as widespread as it once was, does not mean it cannot or will not happen.

The violence of the summer of 2020 was the breaking point of hatred that had been building in America for years. However, the tactics that were used against us were not new. I've led many protests across the nation, and I've seen firsthand radical protestors disguise themselves as allies only to infiltrate our communities and cause mayhem, knowing it would be pinned on us. We were sometimes successful in our attempts to run off such troublemakers who weren't there to support George Floyd or Breonna, but who instead intended to destroy and loot businesses, some of which were Black. This behavior was done in the same spirit of the one that destroyed Tulsa. Both were effective in murdering Black capital.

In order for our communities to thrive, we have to invest in the future. The best way to cast the widest net in doing so is to make sure our schools are providing the well-rounded education necessary to equip our youth with the knowledge and leadership skills to build the foundations that we lay. Sadly, many of our schools are in dilapidated neighborhoods and attempt to educate students with excessive behavior problems. The knee jerk reaction to deal with this is to equip schools with police, metal detectors, and harsh punishments, but I believe the most effective solution is to go the opposite direction and stop criminalizing our children.

In suburban communities, when there are behavioral problems among students, the first move is to address the root cause and provide any necessary mental health care. However, when it's a Black child, the "solution" is to activate the school to prison pipeline with suspension, expulsion, or excommunication to alternative schools. The kid's name becomes tarnished, and children who find themselves out of school often find themselves in trouble. As for alternative schools, many are run just like a prison: students can't talk at all, they have very limited time to eat, and the curriculum comes to a halt while they're kept quiet with "work" much lower than their academic level or no work at all.

The teachers act like wardens, and the dehumanization begins, adding to the destruction of our children's mental health with no means of recognition or recovery.

The mental health crisis is rampant throughout this country, which means our people suffer from it just as much as those of other races. But while the problem might be equal, the solutions are not. We know that we cannot count on anyone but ourselves to fix the problems in our community. It's our job to ensure our children and students get the help they need, especially since we know behavior issues are often intertwined with socioeconomic or systemic issues. When a child is suffering under the weight of such challenges, they do not have the wherewithal to do anything other than act out, which is really a cry for help.

Like physical health, positive mental health promotes success in school, at work, in relationships, and in every other facet of life. Since children spend so many hours at school, it makes sense to have mental health resource workers there with them. How do we implement that? We have to pay these professionals a living wage. However, when you look at the average salary of a school social worker in the United States, it's clear why the turnover for the position is so high. Everybody who works in a school needs more support. That support would mean more support for students. Instead, educators and staff often have to spend their own money to provide supplements and necessities for their students in the classroom, poor students often have to pay for lunch, and cafeteria food almost everywhere is sorely lacking in nutrition. The cycle continues.

If the ideal could be made reality, we would abandon the mindset that the nutritional value of school breakfast and lunch is of no consequence. We would also abandon the mindset that the students in our seats are merely numbers and all that matters is if they're present on count day. We must adopt a learning experience of radical and liberating change that provokes the mind, engages the soul, and provides fun in the classroom, making each student feel like their ideas and presence are meaningful and can carry them through life outside the school's walls.

In the spirit of the Black Panthers' 10 Point Program, we can come together to solve the issues that seem to only get worse decade after decade. Like them, our influence is in our synergy. Our government knows this, which is why they used CoIntelPro to dismantle the Panthers in the first place. They even used our own people from within to disseminate the party. But what is keeping us from creating an organization of just as much power and influence? True radical leaders.

On April 3, 1968, Dr. Martin Luther King Jr. said:

> *Well, I don't know what will happen now. We've got some difficult days ahead. But it doesn't matter with me now. Because I've been to the mountaintop. And I don't mind. Like anybody, I would like to live a long life. Longevity has its place. But I'm not concerned about that now. I just want to do God's will. And he's allowed me to go up to the mountain. And I've looked over. And I've seen the promised land. I may not get there with you. But I want you to*

know tonight, that we, as a people, will get to the promised land. And I'm happy, tonight. I'm not worried about anything. I'm not fearing any man. Mine eyes have seen the glory of the coming of the Lord.[35]

We were striving to reach the mountaintop before 1968, and we've been striving to reach it since. I, Byron Brooks, antiracist, activist, community organizer from the hood, believe our mountaintop has grown so much bigger and so much wider, but that does not mean we stop climbing. No matter how steep the mountainside, no matter how rough the terrain, we must climb with all we have for the advancement of our communities. While we have our nose to the grindstone, however, we need to look up from time to time to see our progress. We don't want to miss the moment we arrive, but how will we know that moment has come?

We thought we'd be further along by now, but still, in the 21st century, we are raising children in a society that tries to feed our children a whitewashed American history while adamantly refusing to incorporate the whole truth and implement critical race theory in schools, even though many of those who oppose the concept cannot even articulate what it is. We are fighting to keep the old basics of MLK and Rosa Parks in classrooms and textbooks against those who are bent on eliminating the truth of our history because it somehow offends them. Theologically, many have abandoned a sound, liberating gospel and replaced it with a prosperity message that sounds good to our ears and for our bank accounts but lacks true conviction and only serves to enrich the lives of those who preach it, not those who listen and are taken advantage of. To that point, I ask our brothers and sisters, have we stopped climbing, and if so, why?

---

35. "'I've Been to the Mountaintop.'"

To climb is to move with effort, especially into or out of a confined space.[36] It's not supposed to be easy, and if you pause too long, you get stiff and set yourself up for failure. We can find hope for our culture, community, people, institutions, and generations of Black and Brown children who will be coming up in this bigoted, racist nation, and we can pull hope from knowing that what we do today has a direct effect on what happens tomorrow. Our power is in our unity and numbers, no matter what racist politicians have to say.

The only way we'll see our mountaintop is if we resolve to become change agents throughout our communities. We all have a gift, a skill, advice, or connections to offer for the cause. Scores of people and groups in the world will try to hinder us from reaching the pinnacle. In fact, societal, educational, and judicial systems are run and/or influenced by white supremacists who will never, ever stop trying to keep us from moving towards our true purpose and potential in this country and in this world. But I am saying, keep climbing. Keep fighting, no matter what. And as you climb, the change will speak for itself.

---

36. Itzigsohn and Brown, "SOCIOLOGY AND THE THEORY OF DOUBLE CONSCIOUSNESS."

How to Build up the Hood

1. Make a goal towards home ownership. If you own a business, strive to own the building. Make sure your assets are insured.

2. Invest in the future by investing in education. Instead of criminalizing the youth, find and contribute to resources for their mental health.

3. Volunteer at a school or youth center.

4. Keep moving forward, even when it seems progress is at a standstill.

5. Become a change agent in your neighborhood. Survey what you have to offer, and find a way to offer it. The hood needs you!

The Talented Tenth

There is, in this world, no such force as the force of a person determined to rise. The human soul cannot be permanently chained.

This quote by W.E.B. DuBois breathes life into my spirit every day. I credit DuBois with guiding the flames of philosophy, culture, and activism in my soul, which he did through his work, *The Souls of Black Folk*. Though the book was written well before I was born, I still feel he was speaking directly to me because the matters he addressed in the book are still fully applicable to the time and experiences Black people are navigating today.

One such matter is the concept of double-consciousness. DuBois said, "It is a peculiar sensation, this double consciousness...one ever feels his two-ness, an American, a Negro; two souls, two thoughts, two un-reconciled strivings; two warring ideals in one dark body, whose dogged strength alone keeps it from being torn asunder."[37] The three elements in this concept include the veil, twoness, and second sight, the veil being the color line that separates black and white, twoness referring to the two worlds—the Black world that largely exists behind the veil, and the White world that dehumanizes Blacks through lack of recognition—and second sight, which refers to an existence that forces Blacks to deal with oppression but simultaneously allows them to glance into the White world to see and understand how they may cancel out said oppression and elevate themselves.

---

37. "The Souls of Black Folk | The Core Curriculum."

It is true that from the time a Black child begins to recognize the differences that so blatantly exist in this country related to race, and this internal conflict begins to arise, even before they can articulate it. Many of us wrestle between the veil and allow ourselves to be scrutinized by society, struggling between who they say we are and we know ourselves to be.

In his essay, "The Talented Tenth," DuBois argues that the best way to uplift the race is to bolster efforts and education of the brightest and most talented members who will then bring others along. Think, "Each one, teach one, each one, reach one." However, while I find the concept as a whole to be a good one, this is where we must begin to examine the problematic elements of the idea. One mark of awareness is the ability to apply nuance, so in all things, we must learn to take the meat and leave the bone when necessary.

It is always wise to explore the context of an idea if possible, and the context of the Talented Tenth is this: while DuBois popularized the notion, the original idea was created by Henry Lyman Morehouse, Morehouse College's namesake. The activist in me recognizes a flaw here because this idea was supposed to be the mapping point of how to save the Black race, however, it wasn't created by anyone Black.

Additionally, DuBois was a proponent of formal education, or those who would be seen in public professions. This makes sense when you consider the elements of the veil and second sight. If Black people are in public positions, we don't have to operate behind the veil. We can be fully visible and therefore put our brilliance on full display. However, the exclusion of blue-collar workers eliminates the experience and wisdom that this demographic has to offer to our community and society as a whole, simply because their intelligence lies somewhere outside an office or classroom.

From this perspective, focus on the 10% belittles the other 90%, and who are we to say the 10% is of more value in this regard? This is a similar elitist view that has kept Black people on the bottom of the totem pole for centuries; it's not something we need to perpetuate among our own people.

Another element that doesn't sit well with me is that the concept of the tenth disregarded our women. History shows us that without Black women, we would not have attained any true or significant advancement in society. Black women have been and forever will be the backbone of our nation and the reason our society thrives. Their courage in the face of fear, their ability to start movements and see them through, their unending support and belief in who we are and can be, have propelled us forward and uplifted many other marginalized groups as well.

They've upheld our communities, empowered our children, educated our people and themselves, and risked their lives while usually going without the appropriate recognition for their contributions. I want to take the time to say, Black women, that you are loved and appreciated, and I, a Black man, am willing to put my life on the line for you. Stay strong and continue to fight because you are our hope, our future, our everything.

Finally, who gets to determine who is deemed the brightest and the best? When DuBois wrote his essay in 1903, the same year 84 Blacks had been lynched on American soil, the thought of higher education was in no way attainable to the majority of Black people. Fast forward to 2023, when education is more attainable than ever, we would far surpass one tenth of our people who, under DuBois's determination, would be fit to lead. According to Education Trust, 26.7% of Black men have a college degree.[38] Once education became accessible, the concept of the talented tenth all but became void, unless we added in a new list of criteria concerning who was the best of the best.

---

38. Anthony, "Raising Undergraduate Degree Attainment Among Black Women and Men Takes on New Urgency Amid the Pandemic - The Education Trust."

But why would we work to eliminate the qualified when inclusion would grow the community at a much faster pace? Finally, if the concept works, multiplication would quickly cancel out the concept of the tenth. Is the goal to grow from the 10th to the 20th, the 50th, and ultimately, the 100th?

In order for us to most effectively fight for our people, we must fine-tune the concept of the Talented Tenth, making it align more appropriately with the times. In its current state, it lacks inclusion. It will take more than 10% of "exceptional" men in our population to tear down the current system of power, privilege, and oppression. Additionally, the 10% meant to help the other 90% should not become a crutch of automatic expectation of assistance for the rest.

In fact, all 100% should strive to do what they can while also learning what they can. This type of attention to accountability and responsibility would cause our greatness to explode; we just need a critical amount of us moving in the same direction. The concept can still have a place in today's world if we focus on inclusion and mentorship.

When we look around and see the many injustices that still surround us, it's easy to say things haven't changed much. But they have changed. In just the last 50 years, we've seen great change in politics, law, business, art, education, athletics, and every other facet of society where Black people were locked out for so long. That does not mean things are even close to where we'd like them to be, but there has been marked growth. Considering this, some believe it is time to retire such celebrations as "The First Black American to Accomplish" a feat, or even Black History Month. I wholeheartedly disagree.

The past opens the door to the future, and each day, we are living Black history. We MUST continue to celebrate our accomplishments so as not to forget where we came from and to lift each other up, knowing we go forth each day in a country where many would seek to tear us down or eliminate us altogether. Though it may be bittersweet that we are still having "Black Firsts," we should never allow the slow move towards justice to minimize our accomplishments or keep us from acknowledging them.

Carter G. Woodson, author of *The Miseducation of the Negro* and founder of Black History Week that later became Black History Month, chose a week in February for the celebration because of Abraham Lincoln's birthday (February 12) and Frederick Douglass's recognized birthday. Douglass was born a slave and never knew his actual birthday, but he chose to celebrate it on February 14. Marvin Dulaney, president of Woodson's 1915 organization Association for the Study of African American Life and History (ASALH) and current official promoter of Black History Month, states, "Those two people were central to helping afford Black people the experience of freedom they have now."

This is true, especially since many in high positions hold the same attitude towards Blacks that Lincoln held when he stated:

> *LADIES AND GENTLEMEN: It will be very difficult for an audience so large as this to hear distinctly what a speaker says, and consequently it is important that as profound silence be preserved as possible.*
>
> *While I was at the hotel to—day, an elderly gentleman called upon me to know whether I was really in favor of producing a perfect equality between the negroes and white people. [Great Laughter.] While I had not proposed to myself on this occasion to say much on that subject, yet as the question was asked me I thought I would occupy perhaps five minutes in saying something in regard to it. I will say then that I am not, nor ever have been, in favor of bringing about in any way the social and political equality of the white and black races, [applause]—that I am not nor ever have been in favor of making voters or jurors of negroes, nor of qualifying them to hold office, nor to intermarry with white people; and I will say in addition to this that there is a physical difference between the*

white and black races which I believe will forever forbid the two races living together on terms of social and political equality. And inasmuch as they cannot so live, while they do remain together there must be the position of superior and inferior, and I as much as any other man am in favor of having the superior position assigned to the white race.[39]

The Abraham Lincoln who is credited and hailed for signing the Emancipation Proclamation is the same Lincoln who had no care or intention to ever make Black folks equal. The date on the calendar has changed, but many politicians' attitudes have not. We cannot be so ignorant as to allow surface-level speeches, promises, signatures, and other shows of personal or political gain to convince us that we have arrived at the equality and equity our people have been seeking since they first landed on this soil. Therefore, we must make it our top priority to continue to achieve, to continue to grow, to continue to excel, and to continue to recognize and celebrate that excellence. ALL of us. It is time that we move as a collective for the benefit of all.

39. TeachingAmericanHistory.org, "The Lincoln-Douglas Debates 4th Debate Part I | Teaching American History."

Agents of Change

We're well into the 21st century, but we're still fighting many of the same battles our ancestors have fought in this county for years and years. Since oppression was written into the codes of operation, it will take many forces over many years to undo those codes and the harm they've caused. It often seems that each time we take a step forward, we take at least a half a step back. There are many theories as to why this happens, but I believe the greatest obstacle to creating change is not the power of our enemies, but instead, it's division among ourselves.

There is power in unity. As we look in the archives of time, history has shown us again and again that white people understand this power. This is why they've orchestrated so many systemic and strategic attacks to sow division within our community. If we're fighting with each other, we lose focus on our oppressor, our problems, and our solutions. Coming together is non-negotiable if we plan to make any lasting progress. When we remove division, we'll finally see the raw power we hold as a unit. This is where the need for block clubs and other places of togetherness serve us. They give us a consistent, safe place to get to know one another.

The tools within our community that are effective at keeping us at odds are many: colorism, poverty, lack of resources, and many others. One of the tools is one of our own doing, the crabs in the barrel mentality by which too many of our people operate. Nothing good can come from envy, but that's the very thing that drives the thought that if one person attains success, their success will hinder the success of another.

We need to believe that success is not limited; there's enough for all of us to have it. But as long as we spend time and energy hoping for and participating in the failure of our fellow brothers and sisters, the longer it will be before we experience both personal and communal success.

Another obstacle that stands in our way is access to resources. How many of our people live in food deserts? How many of our students go to subpar schools? And how many Black and Brown neighborhoods lack the broadband capabilities to utilize the power of the internet any time or day? Such hiccups serve as barriers of entry to the life that's supposed to await all of us as striving American citizens. Additionally, we must remove the term "self-made" from our vocabularies and be mindful of those who rally around us to knock down barriers and help us thrive. I would argue that there's not one person on earth who is truly self-made, as everybody has had help from somebody along the way. Why would anyone want to be self-made when each and all of us can go farther with help?

If you ask most people, they'll say they want to help. They want to contribute their gifts, ideas, and expertise to the betterment of the community. They want to see the community do well, and they want to know they've had a hand in that. However, sometimes it can be difficult to know where to place our energy and resources. The truth is, everyone isn't trustworthy. How can a person know which initiatives to back and who to support? While it's difficult to always be 100% sure of who to follow and who to ignore, consider the following.

Was the community involved in planning whatever initiative a person is trying to launch in their community? Were there any listening sessions? Did the leader take any opportunity or initiative to hear the voice of the people they're trying to serve? If not, then the leader of said initiative could be after clout. They might be trying to elevate themselves. It could also be that they lack experience, which is why they dove into making change without consulting the ones they're trying to make the change for. Either way, be leery.

In terms of who to support, the first question to ask oneself should always be whether the person is grassroots. Do they have roots in the ground? Do they do the work, or do they pose for pictures next to the people who are doing the work? Do they consistently go where the people are, or do you only see them among the people when it's of benefit to them? Think of the groups or individuals who are always seeking out and acting on ways to make things better. Those are the ones who deserve your attention. If you can't think of anyone, just know there is plenty of opportunity for you to become that someone.

The people who deserve our support aren't those who have a nice mission statement on a website, celebrity status, or social media clout. There are a number of celebrities who pretend like they are there to help, but in reality, the picture they paint of themselves doesn't align with the person standing in front of you. We have to be level-headed and intentional with who we connect with and bring in to support our people, and we'll know the real ones by what they do.

It's not enough to be eloquent or inspirational. What matters is what people do day in and day out.

This is precisely why accountability can never be undermined or replaced. All too often, we, as a community, don't support the people we should because they're not flashy or popular. It's up to us to re-center our focus and ask ourselves what we really value. Sadly, too many of us don't know our values, or we don't value the things that truly effect change. When we agree on a set of values as a people, those values become the guiding beacons for who we decide who to throw our efforts behind.

Consider the giants of change efforts in our culture's history. During the Civil Rights Movement, which I would argue never ended since we're still fighting for many of the same rights today as they were during the 1950s and 1960s, our community leaders were clear. We can name many of our leaders who not only gave speeches, but who also initiated civil disobedience, nonviolent resistance, marches, protests, boycotts, freedom rides, and rallies. Tactics of today, as demonstrated by the Black Lives Matter movement, include "looking back," or unflinchingly staring into the eyes of the police, an act that has historically had detrimental effects for Black people. In 2014, activists created the Mirror Casket, an art piece consisting of a casket covered in cracked mirrors that activists carried from Michael Brown's funeral to the local police station in Ferguson, MO, that "forced [police] to look back and see themselves and see what systemic terror looks like for Black communities." Defacing and destroying monuments of white supremacists, social media campaigns, and the sharp rise of positions in the DEI space are other ways activists are forcing change today.[40] All of these efforts, both old and new, have their time and place. All of them are most powerful when we put the numbers behind them.

For these tactics to have the best effect, they must have strong leadership behind them. Who are today's leaders, and what are they doing to position, solidify the status of, and elevate Black people both now and in the future? Our leaders are many. Stacy Abrams, the politician from Georgia who mobilized the masses to vote and works against voter oppression; Bryan Stevenson, author of *Just Mercy*, lawyer, activist, and NYU law professor who founded and directs the Equal Justice Initiative; the late Charles J. Ogletree, author and founder of Harvard Law's Charles Hamilton Houston Institute for Race & Justice; and University of Michigan professors Dr. Charles Davis III, Dr. Christina Morton, and Dr. Philip Bowman, who all poured into me and my journey for change, are only a few.

We must be the change that we seek. Leaders come and go, but we are constants in our communities and in our lives. We may not hold the same titles and positions, but we hold power when it comes to our propensity to see, understand, create solutions, and serve the people around us who we see every day. The time is out for waiting and looking

---

40. Yoganathan, "Black Lives Matter Movement Uses Creative Tactics to Confront Systemic Racism."

to others to lead change when we have the power right within our grasp. Anybody who's paying attention knows there's plenty of work to do.

There are enough issues for anyone who wants to to get involved to jump in and stay busy. The most pressing issues we must address if we are to preserve and elevate our community are poverty, which includes homelessness, underpaid work, and food disparities; a twisted and inequitable American Justice System; what this country inaccurately calls healthcare, which is lacking in quality and access; and education. Look around. The powers that be in more than one state are replaying the strategies of Nazi Germany with their attempts to rewrite history and ban literature that doesn't align with their narrow belief system. These issues are our biggest hurdles.

While these issues may seem vast and insurmountable, they are not. Solving them calls for focused attention, agreement on a plan, consistent work, and numbers. We don't have time to get tired and give up when our first, second, third, and fourth attempts don't yield much fruit. Martin Luther King Jr. said, "The arc of the moral universe is long, but it bends towards justice." We need the endurance to not give up when it takes longer than we'd like to see change. If we lack staying power, the enemy will know that all they need to do is wait us out.

Nobody can save us but us. Nobody is even trying to save us but us. And that's the way it should be. We know what we need and want, and we know how to get it. What we may not know is how to create a plan or strategy that can't be upended by those in high positions who want to see us fail. That's much easier to do when we come together. Whatever it is that keeps us divided–pride, the need to be the one who gets all the credit, a lack of belief in ourselves and each other, or anything else–must die.

How to Be True Agents of Change

1. Refuse to allow division to keep you from the goal.

2. Establish a block club in your community. It doesn't have to be big. It just needs to be a place where people can come together and freely be themselves.

3. Refuse to fall into envy or the need to be the head honcho in your community. Remember the spirit of ubuntu.

4. Don't trust everyone who says they're there to help. Do your research and pay attention to their actions. Actions will eventually reveal their true motives.

5. Work to understand, create solutions for, and serve the people around you.

Keys to Liberation

bell hooks said, "The moment we choose to love, we begin to move against domination, against oppression. The moment we choose to love, we begin to move towards freedom, to act in ways that liberate ourselves and others."[41] Just as our struggles are a shared experience, we can also share in collective liberation. According to Maya Angelou, "The truth is, no one of us can be free until everybody is free." When we think about liberation, we must not only consider that of our own self and mind, but that of our brothers and sisters as well.

In the United States, we are liberated to a degree. We can apply for jobs wherever we want, we can build wealth, we can build our own businesses, we can hold positions of power. Nevertheless, our opportunities to hold positions of power seem to run headfirst into a quota, and many of us who are deserving of status and position will never attain it if we leave our fate in the hands of those who see our skin and decide, despite our achievements, that we are unqualified. Additionally, there are still Black Panthers who are locked up behind bars but should be free.

What is liberation, anyway? Oxford Languages defines it as "the act of setting someone free from imprisonment, slavery, or oppression; release; freedom from limits on thought or behavior."[42] The layers of such freedom are numerous. When we look at the prison industrial

---

41. "A Quote by Bell Hooks."

42. "Liberation Noun - Definition, Pictures, Pronunciation and Usage Notes | Oxford Advanced Learner's Dictionary at OxfordLearnersDictionaries.Com."

complex and see that "Black youth are over four times as likely to be detained or committed in juvenile facilities as their white peers"[43] or that the Black to white prisoner disparity is 4:8 to 1,[44] the need for physical liberation is clear.

When our counterparts argue that we aren't oppressed, but we know the definition of oppression is, "prolonged cruel or unjust treatment or control,"[45] it's clear that Black people are oppressed in this country. If they don't believe it, ask them if they'd want to trade places. We get paid less, our homes are valued for less, we get promoted less, and we are demonized more. The one area we can fully and immediately control is freedom of thought or behavior, but many of us remain in the mindset of the slaved rather than the mindset of the free, which is why we struggle to unify and claim the liberation that is waiting for us only a few steps away.

In 2022, The Grio compiled a list of countries where Black expats seem to find the greatest sense of freedom. This list paralleled the World Happiness Reports list of happiest countries in 2022. According to The Grio, Ghana tops the list for its "Year of The Return" campaign that began in 2019. Black people say they're happier in Ghana because of the "huge Black population, lower prices, and access to the land." Costa Rica is second on the list due to its infrastructure, climate, and landscape that's similar to the southern U.S. Senegal is third because of its safety and flourishing Black expat community.

Panama, which is neutral in war matters, boasts affordable housing, retirement options, pleasant weather, and a strong Afro-Panamanian culture. Portugal is fifth on the list. There are close to 1 million expats there because of its climate and beautiful landscape and low

---

43. Rovner, "Black Disparities in Youth Incarceration."

44. Nellis, "The Color of Justice: Racial and Ethnic Disparity in State Prisons," December 16, 2022.

45. "Oppression | Encyclopedia.Com."

cost of living.[46] A study of these communities can serve two purposes: it can demonstrate steps we can take to bring such bliss to our own communities here in the States, or it can provide a place for us to go when we've had enough. Either way, the change is up to us.

No revolution has ever been funded by its oppressors. We cannot trust the same systems and corporations who profit off of our exploitation to invest, or even consider, our liberation. However, we cannot fully engage in resistance when we're focused on daily survival and overcoming barriers that stand in the way of our essential needs. So does that mean we are stuck? Hardly.

Robust care networks can help to alleviate this pain point, although we must be careful to not be paternalistic in the formation of such networks. Instead, we must allow communities the agency to lead and manage such networks themselves. Liberation requires us to support radical demands for change, not those that are convenient and politically expedient. It demands that we look past our individual interests to consider the good of the whole.

In *The Cross and the Lynching Tree*, James H. Cone writes, "The cross and the lynching tree are the two most emotionally charged symbols in the history of the African-American community." Cone, a theologian, explores these two symbols and their interconnection in the history and souls of Black folk. Both the cross and the lynching tree represent the worst in human beings as well as a thirst for life that refuses to let the worst of situations determine our final meaning. While the lynching tree symbolizes white power and Black death, the cross symbolizes divine power and Black life with God overcoming the power of sin and all death.

Cone states, "For African Americans, the image of Jesus, hung on a tree to die, powerfully grounded their faith that God was with them, even

---

46. "Google."

in the suffering in the lynching era." Jesus represents love, a thread that weaves its interconnectivity through the shared experiences of the cross and the lynching tree. That same love is said to overcome all things. Once we learn to love ourselves and each other, we will move the needle forward with haste.

The components that comprise the human experience are spiritual, mental, emotional, and physical. When we are free spiritually, we acquire a deeper awareness of who we are and why we're here. When we are mentally free, we have the power to seek knowledge and understanding and apply it in sensible, strategic ways. When we are emotionally free, we are no longer slaves to what has hurt us, but we can manipulate that pain to make it serve us for good. And when we are physically free, both in location and in health, we can endure the battle towards liberation and celebrate it appropriately once it's in our grasp.

Freedom within these components bring other types of freedom as well. When we have financial freedom, we have equity. When we are free to create healthy families, we build the community. We build healthy adults. We create a future for ourselves.

In 1907, Mahdist warrior Babiker Bedri, who had just returned to war-torn Sudan, started a school for women. Although some of the very people who would benefit from his efforts initially opposed him, he persisted. He started by holding classes at his home for nine of his own daughters and eight of his neighbors' young girls. Today, the school is the only women's university in the country and has graduated many thousands of women in various fields.[47]

Big movements begin with small steps. We can't do everything today, but we can do something. *Harvard Business Review* provides a workable and effective breakdown for how to go about initiating and carrying out real change:

---

47. "Sudanese Women 116 Years Long Fight for Equity."

Step 1: Define the change you want to see.

Clarity is key. Know exactly what you're trying to do so you can know how to plan for it. Clear vision provides a bedrock to return to when decisions need to be made or when people start to steer off the path.

Step 2: Shift the spectrum of allies.

Figure out who's on your side, who's not, and who's neutral. Harvard Business Review states, "Successful movements don't overpower their opponents; they gradually undermine their opponents' support." This means to focus on those who support you, then move towards the neutral. "Once you start winning over the passive opposition, you're on the brink of victory," states HBR.

Step 3: Identify the pillars of power.

Figure out which powerful entities, like the media, police, education systems, government agencies, or churches, are willing to support your efforts. Once you know who they are, appeal to them by stating the ways they will benefit by supporting you.

Step 4: Seek to attract, not to overpower.

Many movements lose their way because they spend more time demonizing the other side than they spend strengthening and deploying their own. Set small goals at first and achieve them. This will give your efforts receipts to present to those you hope will join you. They'll see your initial success and want to get on board.

Step 5: Build a plan to survive victory.

Ironically, one of the most dangerous stages of a revolution is just after victory has been won. In Ukraine's 2004 Orange Revolution, the incoming team was unable to create a unified, effective government, and soon the country devolved into chaos once again. Secular protesters prevailed in Egypt in 2011, but it was the Muslim Brotherhood that won the elections that followed," writes HBR. Winning the battle doesn't mean you've won the war. It takes more energy to defend a championship than it does to win the first one. Be just as focused on maintaining and building on wins as you are on attaining them in the first place.

The time has come for us to dedicate our skills, gifts, knowledge, and resources to our own community so we can finally nurture it into becoming what it's been capable of becoming from the start. By taking the knowledge and strategies outlined here, we can establish task forces in cities and towns throughout the country and make changes city by city, town by town, state by state, mind by mind.

When most of us explain our priorities to others, we voice love as a core value. Since love is central to who we are as people, then it's naturally central to who we are when we come together in community. The disconnect comes when we don't consistently act out of love. Small changes in mindset and outward actions will equate to huge changes if we perform them systematically.

People will know who we are by what we love. It's important for us to remember each day that while we're busy loving our families, our jobs, our hobbies, and even ourselves, the hood needs love, too.

About the Author

Tupac Shakur once stated: "we wouldn't ask why a rose that grew from the concrete for having damaged petals, in turn, we would all celebrate its tenacity, we would all love its will to reach the sun, well, we are the roses, this is the concrete and these are my damaged petals, don't ask me why, thank God, and ask me how." Imagine if you will, a child destined for failure before even drawing a single breath of life. A child of whom on April 9, 1995, was born a statistic. Not just being born within a Nation that has oppressed its ancestors for over 400 years. Not just being born a black boy full of melanated skin in a society that says he wouldn't make it to the age of

A child literally born in prison, not knowing his biological father. Fast forward years later, and this young man is embodied within the ravages of poverty and homelessness, as he pursues a higher education through community college, and the saddest part of his situation is the fact that his mother told him that he was not good enough for college and needed to work at a factory, hence him being presented with a choice of dropping out or leaving her home. How could such a seed ferment from such oppressive, unfertile concreted soil, and somehow blossom into a rose?

My name is Byron D. Brooks aka "MoSoul" and I AM that concrete rose!

Bibliography

1. The Administration for Children and Families. "Bridging the Data Gap for Marriage and Family Research: Potential Opportunities within the NLSY97," April 29, 2019. https://www.acf.hhs.gov/opre/report/bridging-data-gap-marriage-and-family-research-pot ential-opportunities-within-nlsy97.

2. ChildTrends. "Family, Economic, and Geographic Characteristics of Black Families with Children - Child Trends," March 5, 2021. https://www.childtrends.org/publications/family-economic-and-geographic-characteristic s-of-black-families-with-children.

3. Ibid.

4. Miller, Julie. "BlacKKKlansman: The True Story of How Ron Stallworth Infiltrated the K.K.K." *Vanity Fair*, August 10, 2018. https://www.vanityfair.com/hollywood/2018/08/blackkklansman-ron-stallworth-true-stor y-spike-lee-kkk.

5. "Old West Lawmen," n.d. https://www.legendsofamerica.com/we-bassreeves/#:~:text=Born%20to%20slave%20par ents%20in,heroes%20in%20our%20nation's%20history.

6. Steve TV Show. "#RealGood: Fighting Gun Violence with Love | STEVE HARVEY," September 28, 2016. https://www.youtube.com/watch?v=t4t_XS_byG8.

7. "Education Definition & Meaning | Dictionary.Com." In *Dictionary. Com*, September 17, 2020. https://www.dictionary.com/browse/education.

8. Colarossi, Natalie. "African American History You Probably Weren't Taught in School." *Insider*, June 26, 2020. https://www.insider.com/african-american-history-you-probably-werent-taught-in-school-2020-6.

9. Piper, Kaitlin, Amy Elder, Tiffaney L. Renfro, Allison Iwan, Marizen Ramirez, and Briana Woods-Jaeger. "The Importance of Anti-Racism in Trauma-Informed Family Engagement." *Administration and Policy in Mental Health* 49, no. 1 (June 30, 2021): 125–38. https://doi.org/10.1007/s10488-021-01147-1.

10. Anti-Racism and Allyship 7 Day Journey. "The AAJ Glossary - Anti-Racism and Allyship 7 Day Journey," February 16, 2021. https://gsb-sites.stanford.edu/anti-racism-and-allyship/the-aaj-glossary/.

11. "Guides: Anti-Black Racism: History, Ideology, and Resistance - Oakland Campus: Ally to Accomplice," n.d. https://pitt.libguides.com/antiracism/ally.

12. City Journal. "Poverty and Violent Crime Don't Go Hand in Hand | City Journal," March 23, 2023. https://www.city-journal.org/poverty-and-violent-crime-dont-go-hand-in-hand.

13. Lynn, Samara. "'Black-on-Black Crime': A Loaded and Controversial Phrase Often Heard amid Calls for Police Reform." *ABC News*, August 3, 2020. https://abcnews.go.com/US/black-black-crime-loaded-controversial-phrase-heard-amid/st ory?id=72051613.

14. Bureau of Justice Statistics. "Violent Victimization by Race or Hispanic Origin, 2008–2021 | Bureau of Justice Statistics," n.d. https://bjs.ojp.gov/violent-victimization-race-or-hispanic-origin-2008-2021.

15. Official Georgia Tourism & Travel Website | Explore Georgia.org. "Churches Pivotal to the Civil Rights Movement to Visit Today," n.d. https://www.exploregeorgia.org/things-to-do/list/churches-pivotal-to-the-civil-rights-mov ement-to-visit-today#:~:text=During%20the%20civil%20rights%20movement,physical% 2C%20moral%20and%20spiritual%20support.

16. Walker, Aswad, and Aswad Walker. "Top 5 Reasons Black Millennials Are Leaving the Church." *DefenderNetwork.Com*, July 17, 2023. https://defendernetwork.com/news/opinion/top-5-reasons-black-millennials-are-leaving-t he-church/.

17. Pasley, James. "15 American Landmarks That Were Built by Enslaved People." *Business Insider*, February 22, 2023. https://www.businessinsider.com/american-landmarks-that-were-built-by-slaves-2019-9# mount-vernon-in-virginia-16.

18. Aladangady, Aditya. "Wealth Inequality and the Racial Wealth Gap," October 22, 2021. https://www.federalreserve.gov/econres/notes/feds-notes/wealth-inequality-and-the-racial -wealth-gap-20211022.html#:~:text=In%20the%20United%20States%2C%20the,percent %20as%20much%20net%20wealth.

19. EBRI. Fast Facts. "How Is Debt Different by Race and Ethnicity?" January 7, 2021. #375. chrome-extension://efaidnbmnnnibpcajpcglclefindmkaj/https://www.ebri.org/docs/default-source/fast-facts/ff-375-debtbyrace-7jan21.pdf?sfvrsn=39bf3a2f_4

20. International Association of Chiefs of Police. "Law Enforcement Code of Ethics," n.d. https://www.theiacp.org/resources/law-enforcement-code-of-ethics.

21. Racial Equity Tools. "Plan, Change Process, Accountability," n.d. https://www.racialequitytools.org/resources/plan/change-process/accountability.

22. Ibid.

23. Wikipedia contributors. "Talented Tenth." *Wikipedia*, August 31, 2023. https://en.wikipedia.org/wiki/Talented_tenth#:~:text=Du%20Bois%20thought%20it%20a ,directly%20involved%20in%20so-cial%20change.

24. Battle, Juan, and Earl Wright. "W.E.B. Du Bois's Talented Tenth." *Journal of Black Studies* 32, no. 6 (July 1, 2002): 654–72. https://doi.org/10.1177/00234702032006002.

25. Nellis, Ashley, PhD. "The Color of Justice: Racial and Ethnic Disparity in State Prisons." *The Sentencing Project*, December 16, 2022. https://www.sentencingproject.org/reports/the-color-of-justice-racial-and-ethnic-disparity-in-state-prisons-the-sentencing-project/.

26. "BOP Statistics: Average Inmate Age," n.d. https://www.bop.gov/about/statistics/statistics_inmate_age.jsp.

27. FBI. "Table 43," n.d. https://ucr.fbi.gov/crime-in-the-u.s/2019/crime-in-the-u.s.-2019/topic-pages/tables/table-4 3.

28. "Definition of Tolerance." In *Merriam-Webster Dictionary*, September 5, 2023. https://www.merriam-webster.com/dictionary/tolerance.

29. BlackPast. "(1966) The Black Panther Party Ten-Point Program •," June 15, 2021. https://www.blackpast.org/african-american-history/primary-documents-african-american -history/black-panther-party-ten-point-program-1966/.

30. Lartey, Jamiles, and Abbie VanSickle. "'Don't Kill Me': Others Tell of Abuse by Officer Who Knelt on George Floyd." *The New York Times*, April 22, 2021. https://www.nytimes.com/2021/02/02/us/derek-chauvin-george-floyd-past-cases.html.

31. "The Power of Us: Black Women Deciding Elections | League of Women Voters," September 14, 2022. https://www.lwv.org/newsroom/news-clips/power-us-black-women-deciding-elections.

32. Schnall, Marianne. "New Report On The State Of Black Women In American Politics Highlights Both Progress And Untapped Potential." *Forbes*, November 3, 2021. https://www.forbes.com/sites/marianneschnall/2021/11/03/new-report-on-the-state-of-black-women-in-american-politics-highlights-both-progress-and-untapped-potential/?sh=1ea343c16fd4.

33. PBS NewsHour. "The Racial History of the Electoral College — and Why Efforts to Change It Have Stalled," January 21, 2018. https://www.pbs.org/newshour/nation/the-racial-history-of-the-electoral-college-and-why-efforts-to-change-it-have-stalled.

34. Ibid.

35. The Martin Luther King, Jr. Research and Education Institute. "'I've Been to the Mountaintop,'" n.d. https://kinginstitute.stanford.edu/ive-been-mountaintop.

36. Itzigsohn, José, and Karida L. Brown. "SOCIOLOGY AND THE THEORY OF DOUBLE CONSCIOUSNESS." *Du Bois Review* 12, no. 2 (January 1, 2015): 231–48. https://doi.org/10.1017/s1742058x15000107.

37. "The Souls of Black Folk | The Core Curriculum," n.d. https://www.college.columbia.edu/core/content/souls-black-folk.

38. Anthony, Marshall, Jr. "Raising Undergraduate Degree Attainment Among Black Women and Men Takes on New Urgency Amid the Pandemic - The Education Trust." The Education Trust, December 21, 2021. https://edtrust.org/resource/national-and-state-degree-attainment-for-black-women-and-m en/.

39. TeachingAmericanHistory.org. "The Lincoln-Douglas Debates 4th Debate Part I | Teaching American History." Teaching American History, September 10, 2021. https://teachingamericanhistory.org/document/the-lincoln-douglas-debates-4th-debate-par t-i/.

40. Yoganathan, Nimalan. "Black Lives Matter Movement Uses Creative Tactics to Confront Systemic Racism." The Conversation, n.d. https://theconversation.com/black-lives-matter-movement-uses-creative-tactics-to-confro nt-systemic-racism-143273.

41. "A Quote by Bell Hooks," n.d. https://www.goodreads.com/quotes/8872595-the-moment-we-choose-to-love-we-begin-to -move.

42. "Liberation Noun - Definition, Pictures, Pronunciation and Usage Notes | Oxford Advanced Learner's Dictionary at OxfordLearnersDictionaries.Com," n.d. https://www.oxfordlearnersdictionaries.com/us/definition/english/liberation#:~:text=liber ation-,noun,the%20control%20of%20somebody%20else.

43. Rovner, Joshua. "Black Disparities in Youth Incarceration." *The Sentencing Project*, October 20, 2022. https://www.sentencingproject.org/fact-sheet/black-disparities-in-youth-incarceration/.

44. ———. "The Color of Justice: Racial and Ethnic Disparity in State Prisons." *The Sentencing Project*, December 16, 2022. https://www.sentencingproject.org/reports/the-color-of-justice-racial-and-ethnic-disparity-in-state-prisons-the-sentencing-project/.

45. "Oppression | Encyclopedia.Com," n.d. https://www.encyclopedia.com/social-sciences-and-law/law/law/oppression.

46. "Google," July 30, 2022. https://thegrio.com/2022/07/30/happiest-countries-in-the-world-list-attractingr-black-expats/.

47. IDEA. "Sudanese Women 116 Years Long Fight for Equity," n.d. https://www.idea.int/news-media/news/sudanese-women-116-years-long-fight-equity.

www.ingramcontent.com/pod-product-compliance
Lightning Source LLC
Chambersburg PA
CBHW051214120626
46547CB00013B/1354